Ancient Rome

Discovering Lost Stories from Roman History

Free Bonus from Captivating History
(Available for a Limited time)

Hi History Lovers!

Now you have a chance to join our exclusive history list so you can get your first history ebook for free as well as discounts and a potential to get more history books for free!

Simply visit the link below to join.

Or, Scan the QR code!

captivatinghistory.com/ebook

Also, make sure to follow us on Facebook, X, and YouTube by searching for Captivating History.

Table of Contents

Introduction

The ancient Romans were a proud people. They were proud of their military might, their engineering inventions, and, of course, their empire, which stretched across continents. However, their pride was not only limited to their achievements; it also extended to how they viewed their legacy. Romans took their reputation seriously and believed in the power of memory. In their eyes, to be remembered was to live on. Emperors, generals, and heroes were deified after their death to preserve their legacy. Statues were built, and grand monuments were commissioned to honor them.

To be forgotten, however, was to truly die. It is safe to say that the Romans' obsession with their legacy had a darker side. Indeed, they celebrated those they viewed as successful, but the Romans also had a way of ensuring those they despised or even feared remained forgotten. Known as *damnatio memoriae* (translated to "condemnation of memory"), this was a form of punishment for figures who had greatly harmed the empire and fell out of favor. Once an individual was subjected to this punishment (often after their death), the Romans would do everything in their power to remove evidence of their existence. The individual's statues and portraits would be destroyed, their name would be scratched from public records, and buildings once dedicated to them would be demolished, only to be replaced with another dedicated to someone better. But no matter how meticulous they were in erasing the legacies of these people, some stories were never meant to be buried forever.

Of course, not all of the forgotten history of ancient Rome was the result of *damnatio memoriae*. Many people simply struggled to survive the test of time or were overshadowed by bigger figures, such as Julius Caesar, Augustus, or Justinian of the Byzantine Empire. Few are aware of powerful women like Agrippina the Younger and Livia, who quietly controlled the Eternal City and influenced the decisions of the mighty emperors. Julia Domna, for one, was a woman of philosophy who followed her husband on military campaigns across the empire, yet her name is unfamiliar to many.

Although emperors were on the highest tier of the Roman hierarchy, they were often exposed to assassination plots, which were sometimes arranged by their most trusted allies. These tales of betrayal and political intrigue are rarely highlighted, as writers often expanded only on the triumphs and successes of the emperors. In our version of untold stories, we shed light on emperors who met their end not on the bloody battlefield but through a weapon many thought to be used only by the weak: poison.

While the ancient Romans typically took pride in their success on land, few today are aware of the secrets that the Mediterranean Sea held. The empire emerged victorious in countless battles, but there were times when the threat of pirates pushed Rome to the brink. Pompey the Great, for instance, led an impressive campaign to suppress the marauders, but his story and reputation were often reduced to being Caesar's greatest opponent. The same could also be said about Sextus, whose maritime prowess was forgotten due to ancient historians who sought to forever name him as the Roman Republic's enemy.

When speaking of entertainment in ancient Rome, one cannot help but imagine a duel between two muscular gladiators who must fight to the death. Few are aware of the *bestiarii*, fighters who fought against wild beasts in the Colosseum. These brutal fights were not the only entertainment that the Romans enjoyed; chariot races also existed, although gladiatorial games often take the spotlight in modern-day books and films.

We will explore only a small fraction of the untold history of Rome, from the women of Rome to poisoned emperors to forgotten slave rebellions. The Eternal City might have been built on pride and had a long story of successful conquests and victories, but the stories that Rome attempted to bury truly show us the complexity of one of the greatest empires in history.

Chapter 1 – The Life of Julius Caesar

The Aegean Sea appeared serene and peaceful to the untrained eye. Yet, the threat of danger was always present beneath its surface. The pirates of Cilicia were some of the biggest challenges that one had to face whenever they were on a voyage across the sea. For years, these marauders had built a fearsome reputation. Their ships were as swift as an eagle. Those with little experience in the ocean could only dream of returning to their homeland unscathed once they were spotted and chased by these vicious pirates.

The Cilician pirates were not typical bandits. They were a well-organized force with years of experience. Their wealth typically came from various illegal activities. Not only did they seize merchant vessels and take the cargo that they deemed valuable, but these pirates also occasionally kidnapped those on board. However, the people they chose to kidnap were not random; the Cilician pirates were particular about their victims, as they wanted to demand the highest ransom possible.

There was a day when the pirates of Cilicia found the perfect victim to kidnap. He was aboard a small Roman vessel. The Romans were quick to recognize the sight of the pirate ships on the horizon. Knowing they could not go on a direct assault against the pirates, the crew attempted to flee. However, their efforts were in vain, as the pirate ships proved to be much faster and more agile. It only took a moment until the pirates surrounded them completely. Without wasting any time, the pirates boarded the Roman ship, each drawing their swords to add a sense of intimidation. Fighting was absolutely out of the question, and the Romans were forced to watch as the pirates took some of them captive.

The pirates were eager to make a quick profit out of their hostages. They scanned a particular victim who appeared to be of noble lineage. He had fine clothes, and every movement showed that he was not a commoner. They began discussing the young man's ransom. They eventually settled on a ransom of twenty talents (a sum that was almost equivalent to a soldier's annual salary at the time). However, much to their surprise, the nobleman interrupted their discussion.

"What audacity!" he exclaimed. "You clearly do not know who you've captured if twenty talents is the amount you came up with!"

The pirates were stunned. They had never captured anyone so bold; typically, once the hostages were brought aboard their ship, they would be either trembling or begging the pirates to spare their lives. It was at this moment that the young man finally revealed his identity-he was none other than the young Julius Caesar.

Before Caesar's ship was surrounded by pirates, he was on his way to Rhodes. He was supposed to sharpen his oratory skills under the tutelage of Apollonius Molon, an esteemed Greek rhetorician. In ancient Rome, it was a must for a noble to strive for excellence and conquer knowledge. Thus, Caesar made it his top priority to master the art of oratory, knowing well that it would be essential for his future in the harsh Roman political world.

"I am worth fifty talents at least," Caesar announced, his voice a mix of pride and irritation.

The pirates were initially amused by his outlandish demand. After all, Caesar was but a young man at the time, and his name was not widely known yet. Nevertheless, they eventually agreed to a higher ransom. However, despite his age, Caesar was ready to assert his authority. He planned on turning the tables on those who had captured him.

He remained in captivity—or rather, custody—for eighty-three days, but he was not a typical prisoner. He never begged for the pirates to return him to Rome. Instead, he behaved as if he was their superior. The pirates, somehow amused and in awe of his behavior, allowed him to participate in their activities. Caesar exercised with the pirates and never held back when it came to criticizing their lack of sophistication.

Once, he practiced his poetry and speech in front of them, but the pirates mocked him. Never one to be embarrassed, Caesar pointed at them, claiming they were nothing more than vagrants who had no idea of knowledge. The young nobleman also told the pirates that he would one day return to capture them and crucify them—a statement that the pirates thought to be a joke.

CÉSAR
est fait prisonnier par des pirates.

An illustration of Julius Caesar being taken captive by pirates.[1]

Julius Caesar was known to be a very determined person. His words were far more than just a mere boast. Everything he said came true after the ransom was paid. In the name of eradicating the Roman Republic of violent pirates, Caesar raised a fleet months later and searched for his former captors relentlessly.

It did not take long until he caught up with them. The sight of Caesar with his troops probably widened the eyes of the pirates who once laughed in his face. They now faced the full wrath of the man they had underestimated. Caesar stayed true to his words and crucified them. However, their throats were first slit before being tied to the wooden cross. While some suggest it was an act of disdain, others claim Caesar was showing his final act of mercy on the pirates. They were spared from the prolonged agony of crucifixion. Although one could never be sure about his intention at that moment, many can safely agree that Julius Caesar was not a man to be trifled with.

Caesar's Early Life and Image

Whenever Caesar's name is mentioned, the image that often comes to mind is that of a powerful general whose ambitions and strategies brought his legions dozens of victories across the Roman provinces. Some might even imagine the famous scene of the general crossing the Rubicon, his first step to reshaping the Roman Republic. Julius Caesar was often seen as the embodiment of strength, a man who was showered with greatness the moment he was born. To those unfamiliar with his story, they might even think that his path to glory was a series of successes. Given his privileged upbringing, it is not a surprise that many think he had it all from the beginning.

However, Caesar's early life was full of struggles, setbacks, and even insecurities. While he was a noble, Caesar was born in 100 BCE when the gens Julia (one of the most prominent patrician families in ancient Rome) was politically weakened. The Julians were believed to be descendants of Venus, but this did not spare them from the turbulent politics of the Eternal City. Caesar's father died when he was sixteen. The responsibilities of the head of the family fell onto him.

When Caesar reached young adulthood, Rome had already tasted chaos, as figures like Sulla and Marius vied for control. Caesar was made familiar with danger. Since he had familial connections to Marius (Sulla's bitter rival), he became one of Sulla's prime targets. Caesar had also married Cornelia, the daughter of Lucius Cornelius Cinna, who was a prominent Marian supporter. This undoubtedly complicated his position. Sulla demanded Caesar divorce his wife, but he refused. He was stripped of his inheritance and left with no choice but to go into hiding. It was only through the intervention of influential family friends that Sulla eventually allowed Caesar to return home, though Sulla did not entirely trust him, declaring that he saw "many a Marius" in Caesar.

Instead of remaining in the shadows, the dangers that plagued Caesar's early life and career only fueled his ambition. He grew more resilient as the years went by, and he knew that his survival and success depended heavily on alliances and boldness. Nevertheless, Caesar could not help but compare his successes to those of Alexander the Great.

The Macedonian king was Caesar's greatest idol. Caesar was captivated by the stories and legends of Alexander's brilliance. He knew everything about the conqueror's battles, strategies, and even his ways of inspiring loyalty in his subjects. He held Alexander in such high regard that he often felt insecure about his own accomplishments. According to certain historical accounts, Caesar once encountered a statue of Alexander in Spain. After staring and admiring the statue for a moment, he was said to have broken down in tears. When asked why, he responded that he was envious of the conqueror. He lamented that Alexander had conquered much of the world when he reached thirty, but he had achieved so little.

Of course, Caesar's lament was not an empty complaint; it was a vow for success. From this point on, Caesar's life was filled with the pursuit of power and glory.

Caesar's Path to Greater Power

Strong alliances were key to dominating the Roman political sphere. So, one of the things that Caesar did to strengthen his position was to get into strategic marriages. His marriage to Cornelia was undoubtedly significant. But when she died, Caesar knew he had to secure another bond since that could be a stepping stone to his ascent to power. After all, marriage in Roman society (especially among the elites) was not merely a personal matter. It was more than often a political tool. Therefore, he married Pompeia, Sulla's granddaughter.

Unfortunately, the union ended after a scandal that took place in 62 BCE. Caesar, who was the pontifex maximus at the time, hosted a religious ceremony at his home. Since it was dedicated to Bona Dea, a deity whose rites were strictly reserved for women, men were forbidden from attending, including Caesar himself.

The scandal happened when a Roman politician named Publius Clodius Pulcher sneaked into the ceremony fully disguised as a woman. He was said to have done so with the intention of seducing Pompeia. However, his presence was soon discovered. It was never confirmed whether Pompeia knew of Publius's plan, but the scandal damaged her reputation. Despite refraining from publicly accusing Pompeia of any wrongdoing, Caesar divorced her. He claimed that his decision was a must since, as pontifex maximus, his wife must be above suspicion.

In 59 BCE, Caesar was elected consul. That same year, he married Calpurnia, the daughter of Lucius Calpurnius Piso Caesoninus, a powerful senator. Calpurnia remained loyal to Caesar until his death. However, the same could not be said about him. Julius Caesar was known for his charm and wit. Thus, it should not be surprising that he had numerous other lovers, likely both male and female. Apart from his notorious affair with Cleopatra, Caesar was rumored to have a relationship with Servilia, the mother of Brutus, one of Caesar's assassins.

Interestingly, despite the influence and successes that he had achieved throughout his life, sources claim that Caesar had insecurities about his physical appearance. He was particularly concerned about his thinning hair. In an effort to hide this, he often combed his hair forward—a detail that a few of his critics and ancient writers noted with a hint of amusement.

Caesar's influence shone even more thanks to the political machinations of the First Triumvirate. After being made a consul in 59 BCE, he achieved another milestone in his career when he was appointed the governor of Gaul. Here, Caesar was given an opportunity to demonstrate his military brilliance as a general. He worked day and night to conduct campaigns that not only expanded Rome's borders but also solidified his reputation as one of the greatest leaders of Rome. It is safe to say that his conquests in Gaul were not just a display of Roman might; they were also a means of securing the loyalty of the Roman soldiers. Caesar knew that he would need the trust of his troops to navigate the rough waters in the future.

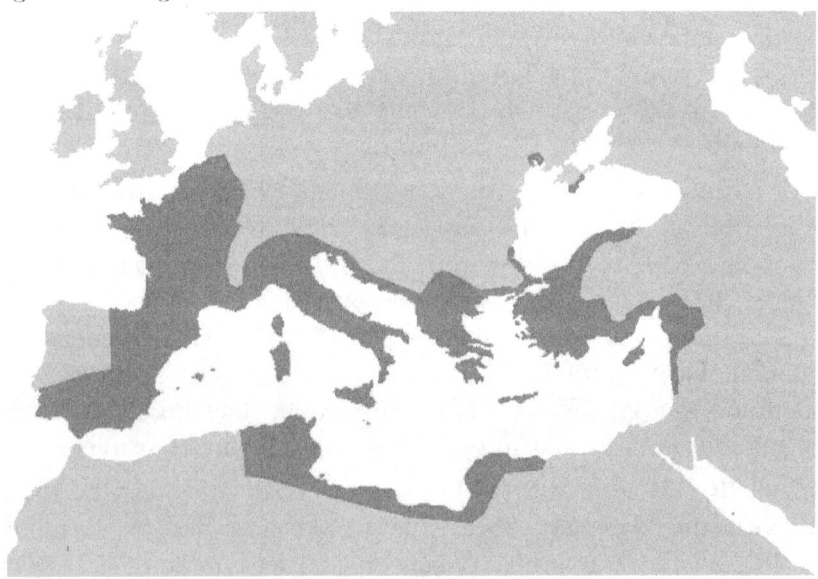

The Roman Republic in 40 BCE after Caesar's conquests.[2]

Of course, like many other leaders in the world—both ancient and modern—their ascent to power was not only due to their military prowess and strategic governance. Some were believed to have been involved in many covert operations. Caesar himself was thought to have been involved in the Catiline conspiracy, which portrayed the dangerous scene of Roman politics in the late republic.

This conspiracy unfolded years before Caesar became a general (it happened sometime between 63 and 62 BCE). The conspiracy was a plot arranged by Lucius Sergius Catilina (famously known as Catiline), an ambitious aristocrat who grew dissatisfied with the Roman government. After failing to become consul several times, the frustrated Catiline began to believe that the government was corrupt. Apart from being disillusioned with the Senate, Catiline was also deeply in debt, which further drove him into voicing his opinions. He began rallying support from other dissatisfied nobles and even veterans who never got the lands they were promised. He even turned to the urban poor, who were suffering from economic hardships. His next step, according to Cicero, was to lead an armed uprising. He allegedly planned on assassinating key senators, including Cicero himself, before taking control of the republic.

Nevertheless, the plot was eventually suppressed. Cicero, who was consul at the time, discovered the plan. He presented evidence to the Senate, which led to the execution of the conspirators without trial. Catiline managed to flee Rome and found refuge in Etruria, where he attempted to raise an army. This failed; he was defeated and killed in battle.

Cicero exposed the Catiline conspiracy in the Roman Senate.[3]

As for Caesar, some claimed that he was among the many who stood behind Catiline or at least showed sympathy to the conspirators. Rumors claimed that Caesar debated in the Senate over how to deal with the conspirators; he was said to have argued against the death penalty and instead voted for life imprisonment. Perhaps it was this action that led to suspicions he was involved in the conspiracy. However, the exact details of his involvement are rather murky. Nevertheless, from here on out, Cicero always had his eyes on Caesar, judging every decision that he made.

Debt was a common issue in the Eternal City; even the elites lost sleep at night thinking about it. Caesar was no exception. Historical accounts claimed that the general was deeply in debt himself, but he was able to use this to his advantage. Instead of using the borrowed wealth to make his life comfortable and live in luxury, Caesar used it to secure loyalty from various allies, even those he owed money to. He used the fortune to bribe those who initially did not see his way and produced propaganda to broaden his network of supporters.

Caesar understood that controlling the narrative was key to winning a republic that was constantly engulfed in wars and scandals. His *Commentaries on the Gallic War* is a great example of how he shaped public perception. His public image was indeed important when it came to cementing his power in the republic. Known for his charisma and ability to speak to the commoners as easily as to the aristocracy, Caesar succeeded in swaying negative public opinions. Through the *Commentaries on the Gallic War*, he was able to bypass the Roman Senate and communicate with the Roman public directly. This way, he succeeded in presenting himself as the hero of Rome, thus diluting the more controversial comments of his campaigns.

His meticulous care for his image did not end with the *Commentaries*. He understood that calculated charm was a necessity in order to maintain both power and the support of the masses. Caesar held games, banquets, and feasts to win over the people of Rome. By doing this, he was seen as their champion. Like modern politicians who create their public personas through social media, Caesar also ensured he used every tool available to shape his image.

Another one of Caesar's aspects that many could not dismiss, even those who wrote about him with full bias, was his exceptional memory. The general was said to have remembered the names of all his men, which undeniably earned him the respect of his soldiers. To the military, this simple gesture of remembering their names was seen as a personal connection. His men would not hesitate to follow him into battle, no matter the odds.

Some might agree that Caesar was something of a fashion icon in his time. He was a trendsetter. When he started wearing his toga slightly differently—he often draped the loose end over his shoulder and arm—the public began to follow suit. Caesar always had a clean-shaven look, although during the republic period, the Romans preferred to keep their beards, as they were considered signs of maturity and wisdom. It was only when Rome transformed into an empire that its people began to adopt the practice of shaving.

In his later years, Caesar again gained the public's favor when he refused kingship. He famously displayed this refusal during Lupercalia, a festival, in 44 BCE. His closest ally and general, Mark Antony, offered him a diadem, which Caesar turned down without hesitation. He knew that the Roman Republic's greatest enemy was the monarchy; therefore, an act of humility was the only way to capture the public's heart.

Internal struggles within the Roman government were common. However, this did not stop Caesar from expressing his care for the Roman citizens. While

Caesar refused the diadem during Lupercalia.'

displays of kindness and care by leaders were, at times, nothing more than an act, Caesar's displays were likely genuine. This can be seen in his will. He left instructions that his villa, gardens, and art gallery be made accessible to the public. He even left his riches to be divided among the citizens. Along with his other deeds, this act of generosity made it possible for his name to be remembered forever.

The Dictator and the Queen of Egypt

Caesar's relationship with Cleopatra is a topic often explored by scholars and history buffs. Their first meeting was as dramatic as it was strategic. Our story begins in 48 BCE after the Battle of Pharsalus. Pompey, having been defeated by Caesar in the battle, made his way to Egypt, where he hoped to earn refuge from the reigning pharaoh, Ptolemy XIII. Unfortunately for the Roman, the pharaoh ordered his assassination instead of providing him shelter. This affected Caesar, who was said to be either saddened by the unjust murder of Pompey or enraged since he had planned on killing Pompey himself. Nevertheless, this opened a door for Cleopatra, who had been exiled by her brother, the pharaoh.

Cleopatra wasted no time in planning her entrance into Egypt and meeting the Roman general herself. Legend has it that Cleopatra had her most trusted advisor, Apollodorus, carry her to Caesar's chamber in the city. Since she was rolled up in a carpet, none of the guards suspected anything when Apollodorus passed through. Once they were in Caesar's chamber, Apollodorus unrolled the carpet to reveal Cleopatra in all her splendor. Although dressed in a simple tunic and perhaps a diadem encircling her head, her charisma immediately captured Caesar's attention.

Cleopatra unveiling herself before Caesar.[5]

From there on, the two quickly became allies and lovers.

Their union was more than just a romantic affair. It was one of the most powerful political alliances in ancient history. Caesar recognized the value of supporting the Egyptian queen. He assisted her in defeating

Ptolemy XIII, allowing her to reclaim the Egyptian throne. Once the civil war in Egypt ended, Caesar remained in the kingdom for a time, enjoying lavish treatment. In another romantic episode, the two went on an extravagant voyage along the Nile.

Egypt was a wealthy kingdom, and by cementing a relationship with its queen, Caesar could direct some of the wealth back to the Eternal City. Cleopatra never shied away from showering the general with gifts. Apart from natural resources and large sums of money, Cleopatra also gifted Caesar with a giraffe, which he brought along the streets of Rome during his procession later on. That was the first time the Romans ever saw such a unique animal.

While his affair with Cleopatra expanded his influence beyond Rome, the relationship also caused a stir back in the city. The majority of Romans viewed Cleopatra with suspicion. After all, in the Roman tradition, it was bizarre for a woman to rule a kingdom. The Romans were also worried that Caesar might become too accustomed to foreign traditions and customs. Their fear worsened with the birth of Ptolemy Caesar, also known as Caesarion, whom Cleopatra claimed to be Caesar's heir.

In 44 BCE, Julius Caesar was declared dictator for life, a title that did not sit well with the Romans, who deeply valued the republic traditions. Caesar's reforms were aimed at centralizing power in his own hands. The Senate had always been a thorn in his side, so he restructured it. He filled the Senate with his supporters and passed laws that curtailed the power of the provincial governors to ensure ultimate loyalty.

Caesar also introduced the Julian calendar, which corrected the inaccuracies of the previous system; this is the basis of the calendar that we use today. Some praised his reforms, but there were also many who criticized his decisions. Although the reforms gave Rome stability after years of chaos, they also alienated many of the old guard who saw signs of tyranny in Caesar's eyes.

This act of power consolidation sowed the seeds of his downfall. The Senate grew restless as they witnessed Caesar's influence grow each day. Even those who once claimed to be his most loyal allies began to doubt him. They worried that Caesar would one day abolish the republic entirely and establish a monarchy, with himself sitting on the throne. And so, they began plotting.

Chapter 2 – The Women Who Ruled Rome

The ancient civilization took omens seriously. They believed that certain events that occurred were signs sent by the divine as either a warning or a clue that could lead humans to the right path. The sibyls' words, for instance, were extremely revered by the Romans and Greeks. As priestesses of Apollo, sibyls were believed to have been given the gift of prophecy by the god. They were thought to have access to divine knowledge beyond human comprehension. Their words, however, were usually cryptic. Nevertheless, the priestesses often received visits from various kings and generals who strongly believed that the fate of their empires could be foretold through their visions.

One of the prophecies told by a sibyl was about the rise of a ruler born from a noblewoman whose lineage was both ancient and pure. When the prophecy spread across the Eternal City, many began to imagine it could be their family's destiny. Among those was Livia Drusilla, a noble who belonged to the Claudian family. Born in 58 BCE, Livia was the wife of Tiberius Claudius Nero, a staunch supporter of the Roman Republic and a strong opponent of Julius Caesar and Octavian (later known as Augustus Caesar).

Livia lived in a period of turmoil. Her early marriage was far from peaceful. When the civil war erupted, she and her husband were forced to flee Rome and live as exiles. During this period of hardship, Livia gave birth to a son, also named Tiberius, in 42 BCE. Little did she know, this was the very child that the sibyl had mentioned.

Things began to change for Livia three years later when she met Octavian. Some said that their connection was immediate. It was believed that Octavian wished to marry her at that very moment, either because of personal attraction or because he had heard of the prophecy and thought Livia was the woman the sibyl foretold. However, Livia was still married to Tiberius Claudius Nero at the time, and she was pregnant with their second child. However, this did not stop Octavian even though he, too, was married to Scribonia.

The future emperor soon arranged his plans. He divorced Scribonia in 39 BCE. On the day of their separation, Scribonia gave birth to Julia the Elder, Octavian's only biological daughter. Then, he persuaded Tiberius to divorce his wife for the sake of a political advantage. Seeing that it could be useful to get on Octavian's good side, Tiberius complied. Octavian and Livia married just three days after she gave birth to her second child, Drusus. This union set in motion the foundation of the Julio-Claudian dynasty, which would rule Rome for nearly a century.

From there on, Livia remained loyal to Augustus. She stood by his side for over four decades and witnessed her husband transform the republic into a vast empire. Unfortunately, when Augustus died in 14 CE, Livia's life also changed. While the great emperor was deified, Livia's reputation was not viewed positively. The historian Tacitus described her as a manipulative figure who played the strings from the shadows. Livia was thought to have had only one goal when she saw Augustus take the reins: to clear the path for her son Tiberius to succeed Augustus and control the empire behind the scenes. Whether these accusations were true or simply political slander, writers of that period never held back in criticizing Livia, painting her more like a villain in Roman history.

Livia was not just a wife to Augustus. Her influence over the late emperor was immense. She was considered his most trusted advisor, and she helped him shape the empire's policies and other decisions. Unlike other powerful women of her time who showed their power openly, Livia thought it was enough for her influence and power to be hidden behind the curtains.

Augustus also entrusted his wife with other administrative responsibilities. He was aware of her capabilities, so he gave her the power to manage the mines in Gaul, which was one of the major sources of revenue for the Roman Empire. Although records are scarce, they are enough to confirm that she succeeded in her role. Her competent administration was efficient and brought immense profit to the empire's coffers.

Much like an emperor would, Livia was given her own court with advisors and patrons. Through this, she was able to gain allies and ensure those who were loyal were rewarded with a good position within the government. Of course, Livia was aware of the importance of public perception. She always had eyes watching her every move, so it was necessary for her to work on garnering respect and admiration from the public. She took the ideal of a Roman matron close to heart and cultivated an image of virtue and piety.

Of course, being a woman of power, especially during ancient times when gender bias was prominent, Livia was not free from obstacles. The biggest of all was managing the succession of the imperial throne. As age was catching up with Augustus, many began to question his successor. It was up to Livia to ensure that her son would be the one to inherit the throne.

Manipulations, plots, and persuasion were common scenes in the court of power. Augustus initially favored his grandsons, Gaius and Lucius Caesar, to succeed him. However, Livia managed to persuade her husband to consider Tiberius. She even persuaded the emperor to adopt Tiberius as his own son. Of course, there would always be rivals to challenge Tiberius's rights, but Livia used everything in her power to ensure that her son was positioned as the natural and inevitable successor to her husband. Although debated by many modern-day scholars, Tacitus claimed that Livia was the one responsible for the early deaths of Gaius and Lucius Caesar. Whether or not this was true remains unknown, but in the end, Livia was successful in placing Tiberius on the throne.

Statues of Livia and her son, Tiberius.[6]

While her son sat on the imperial throne, Livia continued to expand her influence. Although she lived long enough to witness her son's rule, her relationship with Tiberius was often strained. The new emperor sought to assert his power independently without the supervision of his mother. Livia Drusilla eventually died of natural causes in 29 CE. Unlike her husband, her deification was not immediate. Tiberius perhaps resented her influence and delayed any posthumous honors. When her grandson, Claudius, came to the throne years later, Livia was finally deified.

Agrippina the Younger

Agrippina the Younger had a rather rough start. Although she was the great-granddaughter of Augustus (her mother was Agrippina the Elder), the tragic end of her parents changed her life in almost an instant. Her father was none other than Germanicus, the biological grandson of Mark Antony. He was adopted by Emperor Tiberius. Together, Germanicus and Agrippina the Elder were considered the golden couple of Rome. Their dedication to the empire, combined with their nobility and charisma, earned them the respect of the Roman citizens. Many saw their marriage as the perfect union of power and grace. Germanicus had an immense influence over the military. He was a popular general whose deep loyalty to Rome was unquestioned.

In 19 CE, everything changed. Germanicus suddenly died while on a campaign in the East. The cause was a mystery, but almost everyone believed that the culprit was the reigning emperor. Tiberius was allegedly threatened by Germanicus's rising popularity. He might have had concerns that Germanicus could one day steal the throne from him.

Among those who were suspicious of Tiberius was Agrippina the Elder. In a bold move, she openly accused the emperor of murdering her husband. This, of course, did not end well. Her defiance eventually led to her persecution. Agrippina the Elder was sent into exile, and on the emperor's merciless order, she was starved to death. Other sources, however, claimed she starved herself out of despair. Her two eldest sons also faced the same fate.

After losing both of their parents and two brothers, Agrippina the Younger and her sisters were left unprotected, fully exposed to the treacherous world of Roman politics. Despite having been born into a noble family, they were treated with suspicion by the paranoid emperor. Once Agrippina the Younger reached the ripe age of thirteen, she was married off to her cousin, Gnaeus Domitius Ahenobarbus, who was known for his cruelty. Tiberius ordered this union; he thought that the marriage would remove any threat she might pose to the emperor.

Tiberius finally met his end in 37 CE. The throne then passed to Gaius Caesar Augustus Germanicus, who was better known by his childhood nickname, Caligula. With her brother as emperor, Agrippina saw the first ray of light after years of hardship.

For a long time, Tiberius had stained Caligula's family name. In order to undo the damage, Caligula gathered his sisters and bestowed upon them all the honors the empire could give. Agrippina the Younger and her two sisters were elevated to positions of great influence and power. They were given the titles of "Augusta," and their images were minted on coins alongside Caligula—a rare honor, even for royal families.

Coins during Caligula's reign featuring his three sisters.[7]

Unfortunately, Agrippina and her sisters were not allowed to enjoy this period of favor for too long. When one of her sisters, Drusilla, died in 38 CE, Caligula began to transform into a whole different person. Drusilla's death affected Caligula deeply. The emperor had grown attached to her sister to the point where rumors began to circulate that their relationship was unnaturally close. Caligula, perhaps unable to process his grief, turned paranoid, which led to erratic behavior. Rome saw the first signs of political unrest. The court grew tense, and Agrippina was forced to go through another episode of misfortune.

However, it was in this chaotic environment that Agrippina's ambition and survival instincts began to form. She was eventually involved in a plot to remove Caligula, which she did to safeguard her future and spare Rome from experiencing another disaster. Unfortunately, the plot was discovered before it could be carried out. Its failure resulted in severe consequences. Despite being a member of the royal family, Agrippina was publicly humiliated, stripped of her honors, and exiled from the Eternal City. Her life was once again thrown into uncertainty. Nevertheless, this was not the end of her journey. Caligula was assassinated by the Praetorian Guard (the royal bodyguards) in 41 CE. Much to the surprise of many, the throne passed to Claudius, Agrippina and Caligula's paternal uncle.

In an effort to mend the royal family fracture, Claudius allowed Agrippina to return to Rome and reunite with her son, Lucius Domitius Ahenobarbus (named after his father of the same name). Since Claudius did not see Agrippina as a threat, she was allowed to live a life as a minor royal, away from the dangers in court. For a time, Agrippina remained behind the scenes and away from the public eye. Her focus was mainly directed on raising her son.

However, Agrippina and her son could not escape the prying eyes of the Romans forever. Her son soon became a figure of great interest in Rome. He was, after all, the youngest descendant of Augustus. By this point in time, Agrippina was the lone surviving member of her family. Her youngest sister, Livilla, had previously been executed by Caligula for treason. Because of this, Lucius was the only male left who had the right to take his great-great-grandfather's throne. Agrippina was well aware of this. But her experiences in life made her extra cautious. She knew that one small mistake could be disastrous. So, she remained low, at least until the death of Messalina.

Messalina was not only Augustus's great-grandniece but also Claudius's wife. Since Claudius's rise to the throne was a surprise—he was not listed at the top of the list due to his physical disabilities and perceived lack of political ambition—it is safe to assume that Messalina never thought of becoming an empress. She was known for her beauty and intelligence among the Roman citizens, but her reputation changed shortly after she found herself in a position of immense power. Suetonius, Tacitus, and Cassius Dio were among the many ancient historians who wrote Messalina as a figure with insatiable greed.

Other than her desire for more power, Messalina was also said to have had a high sexual appetite. According to traditional sources, she was allegedly involved in a number of extramarital affairs. Tacitus once noted that Messalina once competed with a prostitute in a contest of endurance and won it after twenty-four hours. Although the claim was most likely exaggerated, the story highlights how Roman historians often portrayed her as a symbol of excess and immorality, even by the standards of imperial Rome.

Messalina was entangled in a few plots in the court. She was believed to have orchestrated the downfall of several politicians, mostly wealthy senators and equestrians. She did so by simply pointing fingers, accusing them of treason, adultery, or any other major crime. Because of her influence and power, these accusations were easily proved. Those unfortunate enough to have had their names mentioned by Messalina faced either execution or forced suicide. Messalina was able to seize their wealth and property, adding them to her already full coffers. Her political enemies lived in constant fear, and they could not turn to the emperor, as she would always be around, whispering in her husband's ear to eliminate those who bore even the slightest sign of disobedience.

It could be safe to assume that the bond between Messalina and Claudius was not forged out of love. Messalina was described as a lustful woman—whether this held any truth or was simply a smear campaign by her enemies remains unknown—and the constant absence of her husband made her restless. When Claudius was in Ostia in 48 CE to perform a sacrificial ceremony, Messalina made a move that shocked many. In a public ceremony, she married Gaius Silius, her lover. Gaius was not unfamiliar to the court officials; he was an ambitious man who had always had his eyes locked on the imperial throne. The two conspired to secure their power. Word went around the imperial court claiming that Messalina and Gaius were plotting the emperor's death.

News of the marriage soon reached Claudius, who refused to believe it. However, a certain official managed to persuade the emperor to believe the news; this man was Narcissus, the emperor's advisor, who had long despised Messalina for instigating the execution of many senators. Claudius rushed back to the Eternal City and immediately ordered the arrest of his wife and Gaius Silius. It was said that Claudius was extremely saddened by his wife's actions and drank the entire night. He could not find the will to sign her death warrant.

However, Narcissus was not planning on letting Messalina get away. Messalina requested an audience with the emperor, but Narcissus was worried that Claudius might change his heart and spare her. The vengeful advisor ordered centurions and tribunes to head to where Messalina was being held and execute her. Messalina begged for her life at first, but seeing that there was no hope, she calmly held the tip of a tribune's sword to her breast. The blade was then pushed through her flesh until her soul left her body.

The death of Messalina.[8]

Messalina's death opened a door of opportunity for Agrippina the Younger. In an unexpected move, she married Claudius. This marriage stirred the public, as it was seen as an illegal union. Why Claudius agreed to marry his niece remains debated, but he did change the law, allowing incest marriages. Agrippina successfully solidified her position and saw her path to controlling the empire clear up.

Unlike Livia, who was content with having power over the empire behind the scenes, Agrippina sought to exercise real authority. It was not enough for her to merely influence those around her. Early on, she successfully persuaded her husband to elevate the status of her birthplace in Germany. Known as Colonia Claudia Ara Agrippinensium (modern-day Cologne), the settlement was turned into a Roman colony.

Agrippina also began changing her fashion. After securing ties with the emperor, she was often seen donning the imperial colors of gold and purple, which were typically reserved only for the ruling emperor. She also sat beside Claudius in court. Of course, the sight of Agrippina everywhere in the imperial court disturbed many. In a world where men dominated the government, it was hard for Roman officials to acknowledge a woman's power. Agrippina was also believed to have authored her own autobiography later on, though it did not survive the test of time.

Agrippina remained on the highest level of the hierarchy, along with her husband, for five years. Throughout this period, Rome barely saw any major political intrigues happen. No major coup attempts were made, and no significant violence erupted in the Eternal City. Claudius and Agrippina were busy grooming Nero to be the next emperor. Everything seemed to be going well until October 12th, 54 CE. In her final effort to clear the way for her son's rise to power, Agrippina poisoned Claudius.

Agrippina crowns her son, Nero.[9]

With sixteen-year-old Nero officially the successor of Claudius, Agrippina became the most powerful woman in the empire. She had her portrait minted on coins and carved on friezes. Although her face often appeared alongside Nero, their heads were depicted as equal in size, meaning they possessed equal power and influence. Agrippina was also sometimes portrayed as the personification of a fertile Rome crowning her young son. Agrippina had achieved her goal, but obstacles came in the form of her own son's jealousy.

For years, Agrippina had been sharpening her wits and strategies. Everyone in the imperial court knew her power, and many chose to bow to her command instead of go against her. Nero noticed this and grew resentful of his mother's immense influence. He sought ways to distance himself from Agrippina. He barred her from participating in political events and would occasionally humiliate her in front of both Roman officials and foreign delegations. Nero even went as far as to remove his mother from the palace, leaving Agrippina with no choice but to live in the imperial residence. However, it was not that easy to break her will. Agrippina continued to be a formidable figure in the empire for at least three more years.

Knowing that the only way to curb his mother's power was to remove her entirely, Nero eventually came up with a plot to kill Agrippina. However, assassinating a person of such influence required careful planning. Since she was well connected, a direct attack could be risky and politically dangerous for Nero. So, the emperor staged an elaborate accident. According to his plan, Agrippina was supposed to drown at sea, yet by some miracle, she survived. Desperation soon consumed Nero, and he quickly sent three men to finish the job.

Agrippina was killed at the age of forty-three. Nero denied her a state funeral, which was perhaps due to his resentment of his mother, whom he saw as beyond controlling. The emperor succeeded in eliminating Agrippina, but he failed to erase her memory in Rome. This was the beginning of his downfall as well. Nero's popularity soon waned, and his reign spiraled into chaos.

Julia Domna

Julia Domna was the wife of Emperor Septimius Severus. He was originally born in Leptis Magna in modern-day Libya, part of the Roman province of Africa. Despite being the emperor's second wife, Julia Domna went down in history as one of the most influential women in

Rome. Having been born in 170 CE in Emesa (modern-day Homs, Syria), Julia was the daughter of Julius Bassianus, the high priest of the Syrian sun god Elagabal. It was not a surprise that she had deep religious connections.

Julia married Septimius Severus in 187 CE when Septimius was not yet an emperor. However, his name was not unfamiliar in the empire. As a rising star in both the Roman military and political arena, Severus knew the importance of strategic marriages. After all, he had just lost his wife, Paccia, in 186 CE. He knew it was important to align himself with another influential family. This was when Julia came into the picture. Their marriage brought mutual benefits. While Septimius gained the support of the Eastern provinces, Julia successfully elevated her position in the heart of the empire. She saw Severus as a man of ambition and capability, but Julia also had her own set of abilities.

Julia's influence shone brighter when Severus's career progressed. He eventually claimed the throne in 193 CE after a series of civil wars. Julia was made the emperor's most trusted advisor. She was the one he would turn to for counsel on critical decisions. Her role and involvement in the state's administration was significant. Julia even obtained the trust of the emperor to oversee justice and the empire's financial matters. She was well versed in state affairs, a skill that not every empress could master.

Julia was not tied to the imperial palace. Perhaps not content with remaining in the safe walls of the Eternal City, Julia often accompanied her husband on his military campaigns. Her presence on these campaigns cemented her reputation as a capable empress who cared; she was thought to have a genuine interest in the welfare of the empire. The Roman troops appreciated her decision to stand alongside them. Her presence more or less solidified their loyalty to the Severan dynasty. Julia was given the title Mater Castrorum, which means "Mother of the Camp."

Aside from official state matters and administrative tasks, Julia was also a woman of arts and philosophy. Once she transformed the imperial court into a center of learning and philosophical discourse, Rome began to experience many visits from philosophers, scholars, and artists who hailed from different parts of the known world. The empress was particularly interested in Stoicism, a philosophical school that emphasized self-control, rationality, and virtue. She also appreciated the works produced by Greek philosophers.

The empress even supported the famed Greek writer Philostratus in writing the semi-biographical piece called *Life of Apollonius of Tyana*. Seen as a wise and almost divine figure, Apollonius's life story was composed to deliver messages to readers about the ideals of classical paganism. This work was, of course, meant to counterbalance the rising influence of Christianity. Because of her deep interest in philosophy, Julia often encouraged discussions and debates around these topics in her court, which eventually shaped the intellectual climate of the era.

In an effort to further unify the diverse peoples of the empire under her husband's reign, Julia engaged in the many religious traditions of the Roman Empire. Although she descended from an Arab family whose devotion was to the sun god Elagabal, Julia never failed to show her respect to the traditional Roman gods.

Portraits of Julia Domna, Septimius Severus, and their sons Geta (face erased) and Caracalla.[10]

Julia's life began to take a darker turn when Septimius died in 211 CE. The empress found herself in a difficult position when her two sons, Caracalla and Geta, were made co-emperors. The brothers were constantly at each other's throats, each planning to rise to the throne free from the other. Julia was the mediator between the co-emperors, but maintaining peace between them seemed to be impossible. Their rivalry reached a tragic climax in 212 when Geta was murdered by Caracalla's soldiers right in front of Julia.

Caracalla managed to realize his dreams and claimed the throne for himself. Yet, he hated the fact that his brother's name still lingered in the Eternal City. The new emperor sought every way to erase Geta's memory from history. As for Julia, who was around forty-one years old at the time, she remained a powerful figure in court. Her role was pretty much similar to decades before; she was to advise her son and steer the empire through the chaos.

Despite her counsel, Caracalla was never a favorite among the Romans. His rule was characterized by cruelty and heavy taxation. The growing anger among the Romans soon turned violent in 217. Caracalla met his demise while he was on campaign in the East. He did not die in battle; he was assassinated by his own troops, which were possibly supported by the praetorian prefect, Macrinus, who rose as the next emperor, albeit for a short period.

Although Rome was grateful for the departure of Caracalla, Julia felt otherwise. In addition to facing the sudden loss of another one of her sons, Julia also had to live in a court controlled by her enemies. She eventually took her own life in the same year Caracalla died, marking the decline of the Severan dynasty.

Chapter 3 – Rome's Forgotten Rebellions

A man could be seen staring into blank space. For days, he had been transported from one town to another. His hands were bound tightly in shackles, and he wore only a dirty tunic. The man could not remember the last time he had eaten and drank. The scorching weather weakened him, yet he was unable to leave the world.

The man hailed from Gaul, and his people had just lost to the Romans in a vicious battle. His family was gone, and the man himself was taken prisoner. He was to be taken to the markets, where he would be sold as a slave. From a man who had everything, he was reduced to becoming the spoils of war. He had no value, and the Romans were now free to trade him as if he were livestock.

This was the reality for those who lost in wars back then. The Roman Republic was a force to be reckoned with. It was constantly hungry for more power and land. Wars became common, especially in the unfamiliar lands beyond their borders. Prisoners of war were first marched back to Rome. Those who had been on the higher level of the hierarchy would be paraded during triumphs. They were displayed in chains, and their last stop would be the Temple of Jupiter. Here, the fate of the prisoners would be determined. Former leaders, generals, and kings would either face execution or imprisonment for ransom. Ordinary soldiers and commoners were spared, only to be made into slaves.

Slaves were a necessity in the Roman Republic, especially when large estates (called *latifundia*) began to grow in the countryside like mushrooms. They eventually became the backbone of the Roman agricultural economy, as these estates were the ones producing grain, olives, and wine—resources that fed the population of the Eternal City. But, of course, the booming of the estates came at a terrible human cost. The wealthy patricians needed dozens of slaves to work the fields. Slaves were also a status symbol for the Romans; the more slaves they owned, the higher their reputation. Luckily for them, with each successful conquest Rome achieved came more captives for these landowners to buy. The most notorious slave market was located on Delos.

Just like slavery in modern history, the life of a slave in ancient times was one of relentless toil. Those who were placed on *latifundia* or mines had to work until their body gave up entirely. They were exposed to the scorching sun and the chill of the early morning every day. The slaves had eyes watching them from every corner. The overseers were always ready to inflict pain on those they caught lagging behind. Their status in the Roman hierarchy was the lowest; even freed criminals had more rights than them. And so, it is not surprising that they were housed in the worst way possible. Those who worked in the fields were usually placed in barrack buildings where the interior was nothing more than a prison. They had a roof over their heads, but the food was barely enough to sustain them. Chronic arthritis and the distortion of limbs were common issues they faced.

However, the fields and mines were not the only places these slaves were sent to. There were also those who served in the homes of the wealthy. Referred to as household slaves, their conditions were slightly better than those forced to work outdoors. Their tasks usually included cooking, cleaning, and educating the children of their masters. Nevertheless, they were still at the mercy of their owners; every word that came out of their master's mouth was law, and a simple or even accidental mistake could lead to severe punishment. The only time slaves could breathe freely was during the Saturnalia festival, where they were at least given some freedom.

There was a possibility for the enslaved to win their freedom. Those lucky enough to have a decent master could earn their freedom after years of good service. This, however, was a rare occurrence, as the slaves usually had to buy their freedom with their own money. Nevertheless, even if they were finally free from the chains, life as freedmen was not a breeze. They were still viewed as socially inferior, and more often than not, they were still tied to their former masters through ongoing obligations.

Eunus, the Prophet and King of the Slaves

On the rocky hill of Sicily was the town of Enna, where one of Rome's greatest slave revolts took place in 135 BCE. The slaves had been forced to face inhumane treatment by their owners. A wealthy merchant named Damophilus and his wife, Megallis, were two of the cruelest slave owners in town. Beatings, starvation, and labor without rest were the norm for those who served under Damophilus. Branding of slaves was also practiced, adding more horror to their lives. Megallis was as brutal as her husband. She displayed her viciousness toward her female slaves without hesitance.

Yet, every living being has its limits. The slaves, tired and enraged from their continuous suffering, began to plot for the downfall of their masters and pursue freedom. But, first, they needed a capable leader. This was where a man named Eunus came into the picture.

Eunus was not merely a slave. He was believed by his fellow slaves to have been gifted by the gods themselves. Although records of his early life have been lost to the passage of time, the story of how he came to be the king of the slaves has been preserved. Despite being a slave, Eunus was not tasked with typical work in his master's house. Instead, he was used as an entertainer or "wonderworker" for guests. Eunus had various abilities that could enchant his master's honorable guests, such as breathing fire, telling jokes, and other theatrical performances. Eunus also claimed to have a divine power to see what others could not; in other words, he could tell prophecies. Once, he told the guests that he was approached by a Syrian goddess who told him that he would one day become king. Instead of worrying about his claim, his master and the guests enjoyed his story, thinking it was nothing more than a joke.

It is unsure what Eunus might have felt when his master and the guests thought of his words as tales and fables. However, we can be sure that other slaves viewed him as more than just an entertainer. They saw a potential leader in him, someone who could finally lead them to freedom.

The slaves of Enna, likely just Damophilus's slaves, began gathering in secret to discuss a plot. It did not take long until they decided to seek Eunus's counsel and listen to his prophecies. When they finally met the entertainer, they asked a simple question: what were their chances of success if they rose against their masters? Eunus, claiming that he heard whispers from the gods, told them that the heavens were on their side. He firmly insisted that with the gods favoring rebellion, the time for them to throw off their chains and take up arms against their master had finally arrived.

Perhaps Eunus's words had some truth, and the gods really did favor their decision because the Roman Republic had its attention fully booked at the time. Rome was preoccupied with a conflict in Spain. The Romans had been busy preparing for the Numantine War. This cleared the way for the enslaved in Sicily to make their first move.

With Eunus's blessing and reassurance of divine favor, the slaves who once faced oppression by Damophilus united. There were about four hundred of them ready to strike those who had wronged them for years. They made their way to Enna, and under cover of darkness, they launched an assault. Perhaps fueled by years of pent-up rage and desperation, the town was razed. Damophilus was among their primary targets. He was captured and dragged through the streets of Enna by the very people he had once gladly punished. He pleaded for mercy, yet his cries fell on deaf ears. He was beheaded in a theater by his own slave named Zeuxis.

Megallis was not spared from the wrath. She was killed without hesitation. The only person the slaves spared from that family was their daughter, who had shown kindness and mercy to the slaves in the past.

Their rebellion did not stop at Enna. With their success, the enslaved chose to continue their cause. But, of course, they needed strength and numbers. They turned to Eunus again, although it was not for counsel this time around. Eunus was crowned their king at the very location where Damophilus had been executed. From here on, the slave king went on by the name Antiochus, which he chose after the Hellenistic monarchs of the East.

As king or *cyrios* ("supreme commander"), Eunus did not waste a second planning their next movement. Ironically, his first decree was based on brutality and violence; he ordered the execution of the citizens of Enna. Only blacksmiths were spared from tasting their blades since they were needed to forge weapons. With Enna cleansed from its oppressors—even Eunus's master, Antigenes, was killed—Eunus assumed the regalia of a Hellenistic monarch. This was a move to legitimize his new position and inspire more slaves to take a stand against their masters.

The decision to elect Eunus as king proved to be fruitful, as in just three days, the rebels had transformed into a formidable force. News of the successful uprising spread across the land, reaching hundreds of slaves who yearned for freedom. By this point in time, Eunus had successfully armed six thousand men, all prepared to display their defiance in other parts of Sicily.

Meanwhile, in the coastal town of Agrigentum (modern-day Agrigento, southwest of Enna), another figure rose. Known as Cleon, his first move came after he heard about Eunus's victory. Leading a revolt of his own, Cleon rallied the oppressed and formed a massive force. However, Cleon had no intention of rivaling Eunus as king. He acknowledged his sovereignty and submitted himself to Eunus's command. Since Cleon also brought his forces along, the number of the rebel army grew tremendously.

When the ranks of the rebels swelled, Rome finally decided to take matters seriously. Worried that the insurrection would one day reach the gates of the Eternal City, the Senate dispatched a praetor named Lucius Hypsaeus to Sicily. His task was simple: to quell the rebellion and restore order on the chaotic island. Hypsaeus had every reason to be confident in defeating the slaves. The Roman legions were known to be far superior to many other forces across the globe. However, things quickly turned south when the Romans laid eyes on the rebels.

While Hypsaeus had eight thousand men at his disposal, Eunus and Cleon had successfully gathered over twenty thousand men. Nevertheless, the Roman legions were not planning to back down and return to the Eternal City in shame. Therefore, battles ensued until the Romans were forced to retreat.

With Hypsaeus's legions dealt with, the rebels grew more confident. News of their triumphs spread like wildfire. Distant lands like Attica and Delos were beginning to see revolts breaking out. Those in Rome were beginning to be plagued by fear; not only were they in the midst of war, but they were also endangered by dozens of slave rebellions.

Eunus was fierce in achieving his vision. He led the rebel forces in several key locations on the island. The town of Morgantina (southeast of Enna) was captured along with Tauromenium (modern-day Taormina) on the northeastern coast. They successfully conquered any obstacles thrown at them. They grew so confident that they often performed acts of mockery outside towns garrisoned by Roman troops. Theatrical mimes were among their favorite performances; they were used to mock the soldiers who trembled behind the walls. Each time they achieved a victory, celebrations were held publicly.

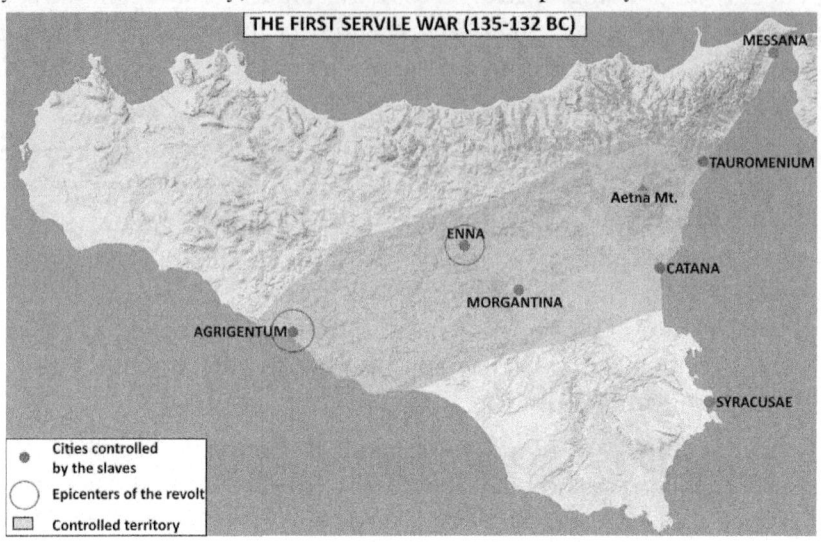

Territories controlled by the slaves under the command of Eunus.[11]

Unfortunately for the rebels, their success would eventually turn into disaster by 132 BCE. The Roman Republic finally chose to display its full might in Sicily. The Roman legions, under the command of the consul Publius Rupilius, successfully laid siege to the many strongholds of the rebels. Eunus could only watch as his forces gradually dwindled. The slave king himself was eventually captured and brought to Rome, where he breathed his last in captivity. While some suggested that he was executed for his defiance, others claimed he resorted to suicide. Whichever it was, his journey ended in the Eternal City, and his death crushed the hope of the thousands who had followed him.

Another Rebellion

Sicily was not meant to enjoy peace forever; it was plunged into chaos by rebellious slaves yet again in 104 BCE, some thirty years following Eunus's and Cleon's uprisings. This time around, a certain decree ignited the first spark of rebellion. By 104 BCE, Rome found itself in another conflict. They were up against the Cimbri and Teutons, two tribes that had proved their might against the Roman legions. With their numbers gradually dwindling, General Gaius Marius decided to seek help from Rome's client kings. One of them was Nicomedes III of Bithynia. Perhaps desperate for reinforcements, Marius did not hesitate to request soldiers from Nicomedes, though the king's reply was rather shocking. Nicomedes claimed he could not help the Romans even if he'd like to. This was because the Romans had already taken most of his capable men and turned them into slaves.

General Gaius Marius appeared victorious among the Cimbri.[12]

Because of this, the Roman Senate was spurred into action. A decree was soon issued that ordered the Romans to free those slaves who had been unlawfully taken; this was especially common in regions like Sicily. The decree was made so that these freedmen could be conscripted into the Roman army. However, this was only the start of another chaotic episode in the Roman Republic.

The decree did not sit well, especially with the wealthy Sicilian landowners. They had profited greatly from slave labor. Freeing them would mean a decrease in revenue. They resisted the decree, refusing to tarnish their reputation and diminish their wealth. Governor Publius Licinius Nerva was stuck in between; the landowners were expressing their dissatisfaction day and night while the Senate was pressing him to enact the decree. He attempted to satisfy both sides. Nerva assured the landowners not to worry about their status, caving into the pressure and freeing only a small number of slaves to appease the Senate. This undoubtedly inflamed tensions and enraged the slaves who had been waiting to be released from their daily torment.

The first revolt of this period began outside of Syracuse. Eighty slaves had united, and together, they launched an assault and killed their masters before building a fortification on a nearby hill. News immediately reached Nerva, but he did not have enough men at his disposal to lay a siege on the fortification. However, Nerva was a cunning man, and he had an idea to bring down the rebels. He picked his most loyal slaves and ordered them to get into the fortification while pretending to betray the Romans. Once they were in the fortified hilltop, these loyal slaves opened the gates for Nerva's forces to storm in. The rebels were not ready to go against proper Roman troops and were immediately overwhelmed. Most were slaughtered, while others who survived chose to commit suicide rather than be recaptured.

Nonetheless, the flames of rebellion had already been ignited. Not long after Nerva's success, another revolt broke out, this time near Heracleia. In this rebellion, the slaves successfully claimed the life of Publius Clonius, an eques whose wealth was only a step lower than the senators. With their victory, many others became inspired to break free from their chains. They murdered the overseers and their masters and raced to join the others on Mount Caprianus. At this point in time, their numbers had swelled to over eight hundred strong. Nerva only learned of this uprising when the rebel forces had grown to over two thousand men.

Nerva turned to the commander of Enna, Marcus Titinius, to deal with the rebels. The attempt, however, ended in failure, which led to the rebels increasing in number and experience. The slave army numbered over six thousand following the defeat of Marcus Titinius. It was high time for the rebels to elect a new leader. They chose a man known as Salvius, who took the name Tryphon, a Seleucid king. Just like Eunus, Tryphon claimed to have the ability to tell prophecies and divinations.

The newly elected slave king knew he had to build a larger force if he were to challenge the other Roman cities of Sicily. He had his men rampage the countryside. They pillaged homes, seizing their resources and welcoming new slaves into their ranks. Tryphon ordered his men to do so until he was able to amass an army of twenty thousand men. Now a full-fledged force, Tryphon did not waste a minute going against the Romans, eventually defeating Nerva himself. With the city of Morgantina falling in his grasp, Tryphon easily gained the upper hand and dominated the eastern part of Sicily.

Another slave leader was busy building his reputation in the west. Known as Athenion, the Romans saw another slave army that numbered at least ten thousand men. Athenion and his forces tried to besiege the city of Lilybaeum, but the effort ended in vain. Not planning to give up, Athenion, perhaps drawing an example from Cleon during the First Servile War, pledged his loyalty to Tryphon, hoping that together they could achieve greater success. Given his fierce determination, Athenion was made Tryphon's general and closest advisor. With their leadership, the slave army was able to capture Triocala, a city that Tryphon turned into his capital.

At Triocala, Tryphon fully embraced his destiny as king. He established a formal court where he surrounded himself with advisors and war generals. He even donned symbols reserved for the Roman royalty, such as the purple toga. While the slaves enjoyed the sight of this new king, for the Romans, this was their ultimate nightmare.

However, history was about to repeat itself again. Like Eunus, Tryphon's reign was never meant to last for too long. He soon died due to unknown reasons, and Athenion wore the mantle next. Athenion worked tirelessly to maintain the momentum of the rebellion. Unfortunately, Athenion lacked in a few areas. Although he was a skilled leader, he did not possess the political acumen of Tryphon and had no gift for telling prophecies. The rebellion began to lose its flame.

In 101 BCE, Rome's greatest general, Gaius Marius, was once again made consul alongside another respected veteran named Manius Aquillius. The two had both fought in the Cimbrian War. Although the rebels had lost Tryphon and gradually lost their grip, they still posed a massive threat to the republic. After all, Sicily was the breadbasket of Rome, and without its usual grain supply, the Eternal City would eventually falter. It did not make it any better that the Cimbrian War was still ongoing; resources were desperately needed for the Romans to win against the invading tribes.

Since Marius had his hands full in the Cimbrian War, the Senate dispatched Aquillius with a full consular army (about 20,000 men, including 2,500 cavalry) to crush the slave revolt once and for all. Athenion was confident in emerging victorious. He outnumbered the Romans by about ten thousand, and most of the rebels already had experience going against the Roman legions. Nonetheless, he clearly underestimated the brilliance of Manius Aquillius. War was not something new to him; Aquillius was a seasoned commander who was further hardened by years of direct combat against the Cimbri.

Therefore, when the two forces clashed on the battlefield, it quickly became apparent to Athenion that their chances of winning were not as high as he had thought.

Of course, Athenion never planned to take a step back. He came face to face with Aquillius himself. He managed to wound the seasoned commander in battle, yet that was not enough to turn the tide. Despite bleeding all over, Aquillius fought the rebel leader and ultimately killed him. With another one of their kings dead, the rebels saw no hope of winning. Their resolve was diminished, and the majority of the forces were demoralized. Those who survived quickly retreated to their strongholds, yet Aquillius refused to let them recuperate. He and his men pursued them without mercy. One by one, these strongholds became targets of a siege. The slaves who were trapped inside did not have enough strength or resources to fight. They had only two choices: death by starvation or submission. Many chose the latter.

With the submission of over a thousand rebels, Aquillius succeeded in his goal. These slaves did not return to their work in the fields or mines. Instead, they were thrown into the gladiatorial arena to fight against wild animals as a form of entertainment for the Romans. This was an execution. However, the slaves were not done with their act of defiance; instead of fighting the animals, they killed each other quietly, with the last one pushing a blade into his own chest.

The Most Famous Slave Rebellion of All

The Third Servile War, which was the most famous slave rebellion of ancient times, erupted less than two decades later. It was led by none other than Spartacus. Beginning in 73 BCE, initial whispers of a revolt could be heard in the gladiatorial training school of Capua.

Spartacus hailed from Thrace and was believed to be a part of the Roman auxiliary forces. His life took a turn when he deserted the Roman army. After getting captured, he was made into a gladiator, living his days fighting men in the arena for the Romans to cheer on. When Spartacus and about seventy other fighters had their limits reached after having to go through harsh training and orders, they decided to make a daring escape. They armed themselves with whatever items they could find, including kitchen utensils. Even though the gladiators lacked proper equipment and weapons, they succeeded in fighting their way out of the school. They struck down anyone who tried to stop their escape and made their way to Mount Vesuvius.

Spartacus was made their leader, and before he knew it, many others joined their ranks. Unlike Eunus, Cleon, Tryphon, and Athenion, who were believed to have had ambitions to overthrow the republic itself, Spartacus only wished to lead his fellow fighters and other slaves who joined his cause out of Italy and away from the Romans' clutches. Once he accomplished his mission, Spartacus planned on disbanding his army so that they could return to their homelands.

However, what began as a small-scale escape later grew into a full-scale war. Perhaps utilizing the experience he gained from being a part of the Roman army and the training he went through in the gladiator school, Spartacus and his men were able to defeat one Roman force after another. His forces were remarkably disciplined and mobile, allowing them to outmaneuver the Roman legions. At one point, it seemed as if the Romans had no chance of defeating the rebels.

The Senate grew ever wary, afraid that Spartacus would come knocking on their door with his vicious fighters. Their fear grew even worse by 72 BCE when they witnessed the immense growth of Spartacus's army. In their eyes, this was not a minor slave uprising; it was a direct threat aimed at toppling the Roman order. It was only after the Senate called upon Marcus Licinius Crassus that the senators were able to finally sleep at night. With at least eight legions under his command, Crassus began his campaign, pursuing the rebels day and night. Crassus aimed to push the rebels to the south, which he eventually succeeded in doing.

The death of Spartacus.[13]

The final battle took place near the River Silarius in 71 BCE. The only way to demoralize the Romans was to slay their commander. Spartacus fought against those who stood before him, charging straight into the heart of the Roman lines. He aimed to find Crassus and strike a blow to the commander himself. Unfortunately, the gods were not on the rebels' side. Spartacus was eventually killed in battle. Six thousand rebels survived the day, but they only lived for a short while. According to historical accounts, they were crucified along the Appian Way.

Chapter 4 – The Mystery of the Ninth Hispana

Gallic King Vercingetorix knew he had to change his strategy after suffering a series of defeats at the hands of the Romans. Continuing to face Julius Caesar and his highly disciplined forces in the open would mean a certain death. So, Vercingetorix retreated to Alesia in 52 BCE, hoping he could use the natural defenses—a

A bronze statue of Vercingetorix in France.[14]

hilltop surrounded by rivers—as a shield against the fierce Romans. His forces had been worn down by Caesar's men, yet the Gallic king remained confident. The retreat was not a sign of his defeat but a part of a larger strategy; he planned on luring Caesar into a siege, and when the time came, he would conduct a pincer attack on the Romans. Then, the Gallic king would summon reinforcements and crush Caesar and his remaining men.

However, the Gallic Wars were not Caesar's first military campaign. The general had extensive experience from years of being on the battlefield. He was able to anticipate Vercingetorix's moves. Caesar's siege preparation was impressive. Not only did he order the construction of a double wall—one facing the fortress and another to shield the Romans from the incoming reinforcements—but he also had the Ninth Legion by his side.

The Ninth Legion was unlike any other Roman force. Their ultimate discipline and battle-hardened resolve separated them from the others. Marching under the eagle standard (a symbol of Roman supremacy), the Ninth Legion was a force to be reckoned with. There was no terrain that could stop the legion from advancing, and their battle tactics were highly effective. Whether they were facing cavalry charges or infantry assaults, the Ninth Legion always showed their might.

Each legionnaire was equipped with the finest weapons. The gladius was used for quick and lethal strikes in close combat, while the rectangular scutum shields gave them great defense against enemy blows. They were also equipped with a heavy javelin that featured a sharp tip capable of penetrating enemy shields. These javelins would also bend upon impact so that they could not be reused by enemies. In addition to the scutum shields, the legionnaires also wore durable *lorica hamata*, a type of chainmail armor.

A modern depiction of Roman legionnaires.[15]

When the Gallic relief army arrived, Vercingetorix launched the assault. Waves of Gallic warriors threw themselves at the outer Roman fortification, while Vercingetorix's forces attacked the inner walls. Unfortunately for the Gauls, this simultaneous assault failed. Another series of attacks was launched by the Gallic forces, yet the Romans held their ground. The Gallic warriors found it especially difficult to break through the shields of the Ninth Legion. They stood firm, and whenever there was an opportunity, their gladii never failed to cut down the enemy.

Eventually, victory belonged to the Romans. Vercingetorix had no choice but to surrender.

A statue of a soldier wearing the Roman lorica hamata.[16]

This was the last major engagement between the Gauls and Romans.

As for the Ninth Legion, their legendary status grew as they followed Caesar in his many campaigns. We can never be sure of the legion's origin, but some believe that it existed decades before Caesar achieved adulthood. Many believe that the Ninth Legion was active on the battlefield as early as 90 BCE when Rome was struggling in the Social War.

We can be sure that when Caesar was appointed governor of Cisalpine Gaul in 58 BCE, the Ninth Legion's loyalty to him was unmatched. They never left the general's side, not even when Caesar crossed the Rubicon, which ignited the civil war in 49 BCE. Throughout this period of turmoil, the legion was at the forefront of the battlefield. The Ninth Legion witnessed Pompey's wrath, as his cavalry pierced through Caesar's forces at the Battle of Pharsalus. However, due to their harsh training and experience, the legion successfully held their ground. Their discipline was out of the world, and combined with Caesar's strategies and tactics, they were able to overwhelm Pompey's forces. It is sufficient to say that the legion played a prominent role in Caesar's success in cementing his control over the republic.

Of course, the Ninth Legion was not without its flaws. In 47 BCE, they were put to yet another test. After years of continuous campaigns, the Ninth Legion, along with the Seventh and Twelfth Legions, were beginning to experience extreme fatigue. Not only were they exhausted, but they were also frustrated by the false promises of rewards. They demanded to be discharged since they had been campaigning for over a decade. To display their dissatisfaction, the soldiers of these four legions mutinied.

At the time, these legions were under the command of Mark Antony, who failed to regain control over the mutineers. Diplomacy was out of the question, at least it was until the arrival of Caesar himself. The general knew he had to regain control of his golden quartet in order to win the fight in his upcoming campaign against the Optimates (Pompey's supporters) in Africa. Yet, Caesar had little in his coffers; the general could not offer money so that the men would reenlist. So, he resorted to a speech.

It was said that the legions went silent the moment they saw Caesar standing before them. He began his speech by addressing the men not as soldiers but as citizens, which signaled to them that they had been discharged. He questioned their loyalty to the republic and acknowledged the fact that he owed them their pay. He told them that he would hold on to his promise and pay them what was due after he returned from the African campaign. He spoke as if he no longer had plans on bringing his four favorite legions—the ones that had stood by his side for so long—with him to Africa. Caesar also threatened to decimate the entire Ninth Legion (a rare punishment in the military where every tenth man was executed).

The soldiers were disheartened by his speech. How could they let their commander charge onto the battlefield without them? They began surrounding Caesar and asked for forgiveness. They begged for the commander to spare the Ninth Legion. The legionnaires even expressed their desperate wish to be reinstated. While Caesar first feigned indifference, he changed his mind when the legionnaires agreed to hand him the names of those who instigated the mutiny. They were then executed.

Having been narrowly spared by Caesar, the Ninth Legion continued to be on his side throughout the rest of his upcoming campaigns. When Caesar was assassinated in 44 BCE, the Ninth Legion continued its service under Octavian in his quest to rise as the first Roman emperor. Perhaps one of the legion's biggest contributions under the emperor was their involvement in the Cantabrian Wars (27–19 BCE).

These wars were some of the most challenging ones under Augustus's reign. The Cantabri and Astures tribes resisted Augustus's rule. They resorted to guerilla tactics, which, more often than not, managed to overcome the Romans. Despite the Ninth Legion being seasoned by many decades of warfare, the difficult terrain and unconventional warfare of the Cantabrian forces posed a great challenge to them. Nevertheless, the legionnaires were known for their ability to hold their formation and respond quickly to an enemy ambush. Combined with their discipline, the Romans eventually won the day. The legion's act of valor in Hispania was recognized by Augustus, who bestowed upon them the honorary title Legio IX Hispana. From here on, the Ninth Hispana was stationed in Spain to assist the Romans in asserting their control over the newly conquered territories.

The legion continued to contribute to the empire for years to come. In 20 CE, the Ninth Hispana was dispatched to North Africa, where they were put under the command of Gaius Fulvius. Their mission was to join the Third Augustan Legion and assist in suppressing a rebellion. Led by Tacfarinas (a former Roman soldier-turned-leader of the Berber Musulamii tribe), the rebellion had been a thorn in the side of the empire. Their guerrilla tactics had been disrupting the settlements and supply lanes of the Romans. The arrival of the Ninth Hispana was supposed to contribute to the Romans' success.

However, things didn't go as planned. A centurion of the Ninth Hispana, Decrius, took a cohort of 480 men and launched a direct assault against Tacfarinas's forces. The Numidian warriors proved to be faster than the Roman soldiers; they managed to evade their attacks and swiftly counter their slashes. Although Decrius fought bravely, he was eventually killed in battle. The defeat was humiliating for the Romans to the point where the Ninth Hispana again faced the threat of decimation. Nevertheless, the legion regrouped and launched a successful counterattack. Tacfarinas was forced to retreat into the desert and never succeeded in reclaiming victory against the Romans.

The Ninth Hispana also survived to witness the unexpected rise of Emperor Claudius and joined his campaign of invading Britain in 43 CE. Little is recorded about their exact activities during this time in Britain until 60 CE when the Boudican revolt surfaced.

Led by Boudica, the queen of the Iceni tribe, it all began with the betrayal of Suetonius Paulinus, the Roman governor of Britain at the time. Not only did he annex the Iceni territory outright (the late Iceni king had left his kingdom jointly to his two daughters and the Roman emperor), but the Romans also seized the Iceni tribe's resources and wealth. The final straw came when Boudica was publicly flogged while her daughters were viciously raped by Roman soldiers. From here on, Boudica worked to unite several tribes under her banner and launched several attacks on Roman settlements.

A statue of Boudica and her daughters in London.[17]

The Ninth Hispana was then dispatched to Camulodunum (modern-day Colchester, Essex) under the command of Petillius Cerialis. During their march, four cohorts were suddenly ambushed by Boudica's forces. Driven by rage, the Britons quickly overwhelmed the Romans. Since they were outnumbered, slaughter was inevitable; nearly all of the infantry fell. Only Cerialis and a few cavalry narrowly escaped. The loss was so massive that the Ninth Hispana had to be reinforced with two thousand men from Legio XXI Rapax.

This was not the end of the famous legion. They remained in action, serving in Britain for several more decades. Their worst challenge came in the late 1st century when the Caledonians (tribes from the north of what is now Scotland) began to show their teeth. The Romans, ever hungry for more territories, were encroaching on their lands. To retaliate, the Caledonians raided multiple Roman outposts and settlements. The Romans were left with no choice but to launch another campaign aimed at crushing the tribes. Led by governor Gnaeus Julius Agricola, several legions, including the Ninth Hispana, marched north in 77 CE.

On one particular night, the Caledonians launched a surprise raid on the Ninth Hispana's camp. This wreaked havoc across the camp, and the Roman soldiers scrambled to get their weapons and hold their ground. For a moment, it seemed as if it was the last time the legion would see action. However, perhaps thanks to Agricola's quick maneuvering, he was able to get reinforcements from the other legions nearby. The Romans managed to repel the Caledonians and secure the camp.

Victory was again awarded to the Romans at the Battle of Mons Graupius in 83 CE, allowing Rome to solidify its control over much of Britain, though the full conquest of the Caledonians was not yet complete. Agricola intended to launch a second invasion to get his hands on the northern territories. However, he was recalled to the Eternal City by Emperor Domitian in 85 CE, as he feared that Agricola's rising popularity would pose a threat to his rule. Because of this, the Roman campaign in northern Britain never got its ending.

The situation in the region became ever precarious under Emperor Hadrian, who rose to power in 117 CE. Hadrian was well known for desiring peace over war. Instead of launching invasion campaigns like his predecessors, the emperor focused on fortifying Rome's frontiers. Hoping to keep the Caledonians at bay, he issued the construction of Hadrian's Wall in 122 CE, which stretched across the width of northern Britain. Many suggest the construction was the result of a certain dark event that took place in the Roman military: the end of the Ninth Hispana.

One theory claimed that the Ninth Hispana met its doom when the men were lured into a trap by the Caledonians. Knowing that Hadrian would always choose the path of peace, the Caledonians were thought to have invited the Romans into a peaceful meeting to discuss terms. The commander of the Ninth Legion, believing that it was an opportunity to finally end the hostilities at the northern frontier and also a chance to earn favor from the peace-loving emperor, agreed to the meeting. Being based at Eburacum (modern-day York) at the time, the legion marched north into Caledonia, where the tribe had set up a meeting point in a rather remote location.

Unsurprisingly, peace was never an option in the eyes of the Caledonians. The Ninth Legion was welcomed with an ambush. Being far from their reinforcements, the legion faced merciless slaughter. Their sacred eagle, which they had sworn to protect with all their might, fell to the ground, and none of the legionnaires were left to pick it up. While some said the Caledonians killed every last one of them, others suggested there were survivors, though their honor was shredded into so many pieces that they were engulfed by shame to recall the event.

By 120 CE, mentions of the Ninth Hispana had vanished completely from the Roman military records. Two years later, another legion was created. Known as the Sixth Victrix, this legion replaced the Ninth Legion. For centuries, the theory that the Ninth Hispana had been removed by the Caledonians stood. The Roman legions were the primary builders of Hadrian's Wall, but interestingly, the Ninth was the only legion that did not participate in its construction. It is hard to dismiss that it was a mere coincidence that the legion mysteriously disappeared right before Hadrian's visit to Britain and his commission to construct his famous wall. This particular theory is also further supported by the discovery of inscriptions bearing the legion's name in York, where they were stationed before meeting the Caledonians. In 1886, the world was shocked by another discovery. A bronze Roman eagle, believed to be the imperial standard of the lost legion, was found in Silchester.

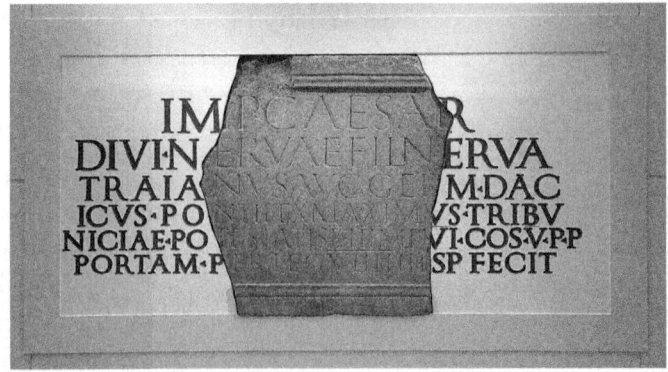

The inscription bearing the legion's name discovered in York.[18]

Of course, there is another theory that suggests otherwise. Some claim the Ninth did not meet their fate in Britain after all. This was due to another archaeological discovery that uncovered inscriptions with the words "Ninth Legion" and "Vex Brit" (which stands for Vexillation Britannica, a detachment of the British Ninth) in Nijmegen, the Netherlands. These findings led scholars to argue that the legion might have been relocated to the Rhine to defend the northern frontier of the empire from the Germanic tribes. Whether or not this is true remains unclear.

Another possibility is that the Ninth might have sealed their fate in 132 CE during the Second Jewish Revolt (also known as the Bar Kokhba Revolt). Since the revolt in Judea was named the most destructive catastrophe to ever happen in the Roman Empire at that time, several legions were deployed to defeat the rebels. The Ninth could have been reassigned to the East and been defeated in battle. However, there is no concrete evidence to support this theory.

If the men of the Ninth Legion were not annihilated during the revolt in Judea, it could be plausible that they fell at the hands of the Parthians. Roman-controlled territories in the East, including Armenia and Syria, were invaded by the Parthian Empire in 161 CE. This undoubtedly sparked a major conflict between the two colossal powers. When several Roman legions were dispatched to defend the empire from the Parthians, the Ninth could have been one of them, though they were among the unlucky ones. The Parthians were exceptionally skilled in mounted warfare and archery, so it was not impossible for the Ninth to have been destroyed by them. However, like the theory where they fell in Judea, this particular theory is nothing more than speculation.

What we can be sure of is that the Ninth Legion completely disappeared from the official Roman record starting from 120 CE. The reason behind this remains a mystery. Apart from being a topic of study by scholars, the disappearance of the Ninth has also given ideas to those in the entertainment industry. They fill the gaps with speculative narratives and different scenes of battles toward the end of their story. The 2010 film *Centurion*, for example, depicted the Ninth Hispana taking its final stand against the Caledonians.

Rosemary Sutcliff wrote and published a fictional book inspired by the mystery of the Ninth Hispana. It follows a Roman officer named Marcus Flavius Aquila, whose task was to recover the lost eagle of the

Ninth Hispana. This piece of fiction drew inspiration from the theory that the legion was wiped out by the northern tribes. This novel was also adapted into a film in 2011, bringing the history of the Ninth Hispana to a new generation of viewers. Despite the lack of records, the legacy of the Ninth Hispana has been successfully immortalized.

Chapter 5 – Conspiracies in the Senate

Caesar woke up slightly earlier than usual. His dreams last night gave him an uneasy feeling, but he chose to brush it off. As he got ready for another day, his wife, Calpurnia, approached. She appeared to be far more disturbed than Caesar, as she herself had been troubled by nightmares of her husband's demise.

"Stay," she said, her voice almost like a whisper. "Don't go to the Senate meeting today. Your blood, Caesar. I see it streaming down the steps of the Senate."

Caesar was moved by her distress, but he was not highly superstitious like a typical Roman usually was. He assured his wife that nothing would happen to him. He had, after all, survived decades of war.

"The Senate will not wait for me, my dear," he responded before leaving.

Caesar made his way through the streets and passed by the Temple of Jupiter. He suddenly remembered the words of a certain soothsayer who approached him during a triumph. "Beware the Ides of March" was what he said. But Caesar had so many things on his plate that he chose not to think about it further.

Meanwhile, in the Senate House, Cassius could be seen pacing back and forth. He was looking forward to this day, yet he had to be more vigilant than usual. He tightened his grasp around the small dagger hidden beneath his toga and looked around at his fellow conspirators, namely, Casca, Brutus, and Decimus. Once they met, they exchanged looks. They knew there was no turning back. Today was the day to save the republic from continuing to bow down to a dictator.

The Roman Senate had always been a center of plots and assassinations. The Senate was an advisory body and was once regarded as the cradle of the Roman Republic. It possessed a significant influence over every aspect of the Eternal City, from legislative decisions to foreign policy to military affairs. But, of course, as the republic expanded its influence and territories, its political landscape grew more complex. Many senators, driven by greed, sought to outmaneuver one another just so they could have more control. Alliances frequently shifted, and loyalty meant almost nothing. Debates were, at times, skipped, as the senators preferred tools like assassinations, purges, proscriptions, or exiles to eliminate their rivals.

Cassius claimed to be a staunch defender of Roman liberty. Therefore, it was not a surprise that he had always viewed Caesar with disdain. His rise as dictator for life meant the erosion of republic values. In his eyes, Rome would certainly crumble under Caesar, whose thirst for power would only keep growing. If Caesar came out of the meeting alive, he could only sit and watch as the dictator used his absolute authority to render the Senate powerless and, with it, the concept of Roman democracy.

The same could be said about Cassius, who would do anything to see Caesar's downfall. In fact, he was the one who planted the seeds of discontent, especially in Brutus. Although it was said that Brutus loved Caesar—the dictator was not only his mentor but a father figure—his love for the republic ran deeper. He grew up listening to stories of Roman virtue, and he idolized men who never hesitated to risk their lives for the sake of freedom. True, Caesar declined the crown thrice, but he continued to display his ultimate power over Rome. The idea that Caesar's rule might put that legacy to an end made him restless. Cassius saw this wariness in Brutus's eyes and saw an opportunity to plant the seeds of doubt in his mind.

"You are the descendant of Lucius Junius Brutus, the one who bravely expelled the last king of Rome!" Cassius might have said. "How could you stand idly by as Caesar crowns himself the ruler of our beloved republic?"

Brutus eventually understood Cassius's intentions, and he agreed with him; the Eternal City must rid itself of Caesar if it were to survive.

The great dictator finally arrived with his customary grandeur. He made his way through the Porticus of Pompey and entered the Senate, where he was met with murmurs of the senators who were beginning to quiet down as he entered. They watched him stride forward, his regal purple toga brushing the stone floor. The silence in the air was heavy. Suddenly, as if they had an urgent matter to discuss, several of the conspirators rose and encircled Caesar. They greeted the dictator warmly, though their expressions were cold. Caesar attended to them, exchanging pleasantries as they guided him toward his golden seat.

Then, Tillius Cimber rose and approached the dictator. Claiming he had urgent matters to discuss, Caesar immediately shifted his entire focus onto him. The senator quickly begged him to recall his exiled brother, and Caesar firmly dismissed his request. Cimber, who had perhaps already rehearsed this motion the night before, held his hand out, reaching the dictator as if to plead further. In a sudden move, he pulled Caesar's toga down from his shoulders. Little did the dictator know that this was a signal.

The assassination of Julius Caesar.[19]

Casca was the first to unveil his dagger. His blade sliced into the mighty dictator's flesh. Stunned by both pain and treachery, Caesar glanced at his first assailant and attempted to fend off the upcoming blow. However, his effort was in vain, as Casca was not the only one to have stepped forward. One by one, the other conspirators lunged forward, their daggers slicing his torso brutally. Blood quickly spilled on the marble floor, pooling around his feet. Caesar, a man who had survived dozens of battlefields, tried to get on his feet, but his strength was clearly fading away.

Shakespeare described the incident vividly in his play. The dictator staggered, hoping he could at least take a final look at the faces who betrayed him, the same men he had trusted and whom he called his friends. One face made his eyes widen.

"Et tu, Brute?" he whispered.

The man he had loved and mentored as a son slowly approached the already dying dictator with his dagger drawn. Brutus gifted the dictator with the final blow. Caesar collapsed, his lifeless body slumping to the ground. The only thing that could be heard was the ragged breathing of the conspirators.

The soothsayer was right all along. The Ides of March had come and gone, as had Julius Caesar. The conspirators thought they could finally breathe easy now that the tyrannical ruler had died. They thought they had spared the Senate from its doom. Yet, Caesar's death did not restore the Roman Republic like the conspirators had hoped for. Instead, it plunged the Eternal City into chaos. Some praised Brutus and Cassius, seeing them as liberators, but the public viewed them as nothing more than traitors.

The streets mourned Caesar. Caesar's most loyal ally, Mark Antony, displayed his grief. Not only did he dress in mourning attire for a period of time, but the war general also refused to shave. Antony further expressed his grief during his famous funeral oration, where he showed to the public Caesar's blood-stained toga. This was also the time when he read Caesar's will and emphasized the Senate's betrayal. The general was attempting to ignite the public's fury and direct their rage toward the conspirators, which eventually worked, as Rome witnessed another civil war.

Mark Antony, Octavian, and Lepidus formed the Second Triumvirate with a goal to hunt down each of the conspirators. Brutus and Cassius paid the ultimate price at the Battle of Philippi, but peace for Rome was still far from reach. When Octavian and Antony's fragile alliance finally came to an end, the two fought each other, plunging the already shattered republic into further conflict. It was only when Octavian rose as Emperor Augustus that Rome began to see the first light of the Pax Romana.

The Ultimate Danger of Those Who Wore the Purple Toga

Although the emperor held supreme authority now that the republic was a thing of the past, senators, generals, and especially the imperial bodyguards (known as the Praetorian Guard) were still considered key players in the treacherous game of Roman politics. Aside from keeping a close eye on the borders and neighboring tribes in case there were revolts or invasions, Roman emperors had to watch out for those closest to them. Emperor Caligula was among the many Roman emperors who failed to do so; he was assassinated in 41 CE by those who were tasked with keeping him safe.

At the very beginning, Caligula's rise to the throne was warmly celebrated by nearly everyone. He came from a distinguished family. His father was Germanicus, one of the greatest Roman generals. He was admired by both the legionnaires and the common people, so many held high hopes for the new emperor. After all, the Romans had suffered under his predecessor, Emperor Tiberius, who was popularly known for his paranoia, absence, and assassinations. Corruption was common under Tiberius, and the Senate was nothing more than just puppets.

Map showing the extent of the empire. (Red - Italy and Roman provinces. Blue - Independent countries. Yellow - Client states. Magenta - Seized by Caligula. Purple - Former Roman provinces made client states by Caligula).[20]

So, when Caligula sat on the throne, he was expected to cleanse the Eternal City of its misfortunes and terror, which he successfully did in the first few months of his reign. Not only did he set everyone free who had been wrongfully imprisoned by Tiberius, but Caligula also wasted no time in pleasing the public. He abolished the harsh taxes that had long dragged his citizens down and used his newly acquired wealth on games and public spectacles. In just a few weeks, Caligula had earned the admiration of the masses. However, things took a sharp turn when the emperor suddenly fell ill.

Although he recovered from the mysterious illness, he seemed to become a different person. What began as signs of eccentricity soon spiraled into full-blown madness. He turned from an honorable and benevolent leader into a tyrant. Policies changed based on his mood swings, and his behavior turned increasingly erratic and cruel as the days passed. He once declared himself a god. It was common for Roman leaders to be deified, but this only happened after their death. Caligula went as far as to demand his subjects worship him. Caligula squandered the empire's coffers by commissioning personal projects, be it his own statues and palaces or the construction of ships for his own entertainment. There were also accounts that told how the emperor, disappointed and enraged with the senators, threatened to make his horse (known as Incitatus) a member of the Senate. He even took pleasure in mocking and humiliating the senators. It was almost like Tiberius's paranoia was contagious. Caligula often purged his government, with the senators and other aristocrats either facing execution or forced suicide.

This combination of paranoia, cruelty, and madness sealed his fate. The Senate seethed under his erratic reign, but the senators were not the ones who hit the final nail in his coffin. It was the Praetorian Guard.

The Praetorian Guard was an elite unit established by Rome's first emperor. Initially, their task was to protect the emperor, but as time went by, this prestigious unit became a significant force in its own right. Some might even describe them as a double-edged sword; they could either make or break emperors. Their loyalty could be bought, but it was far easier to displease them, which could make them extremely deadly.

Caligula had repeatedly abused them. The respected Praetorian commander, Cassius Chaerea, was among the men who had experienced the emperor's erratic behavior firsthand. Chaerea was publicly mocked and belittled more than once. Caligula would often insult his masculinity and refer to him with derogatory names such as *effeminatus*, which implied effeminacy. Since the commander had a rather soft or high-pitched voice, the emperor never held back from making crude jokes about how he sounded. In the ancient Roman culture, personal honor, especially for soldiers, was of immense importance. Caligula's abuse of power and mistreatment contributed to Chaerea's desire for revenge.

The conspiracy took place during the Palatine Games (also known as the Secular Games) on January 24th, 41 CE. The unsuspecting Caligula was first lured into a corridor beneath Palatine Hill, away from the eyes of the public. Once the emperor arrived, the members of the Praetorian Guard ambushed him. Caught off guard, Caligula attempted to flee, but Chaerea was quick enough to stab Caligula in the neck. As if mirroring the assassination of Julius Caesar centuries before, the other conspirators wasted no time in joining in, each leaving a wound on the emperor. The emperor was not the only victim of the conspiracy; his wife, Caesonia, and their infant daughter were also murdered to prevent any possible claim to the throne.

Caligula's assassination.[21]

With the throne left vacant, the Senate hoped to reassert its power. However, the senators knew they could not be that ambitious without the support of the military. At the same time, the Praetorian Guard had another plan. Although the blood of Caligula was on their hands, they had no intention of erasing the imperial system. They turned to one particular candidate to replace the mad emperor: Claudius, Caligula's paternal uncle. This move surprised many, as none expected Claudius to ever wear the wreath. He was kept on the fringes of politics largely due to his perceived physical disabilities (a limp and a speech impediment). Many saw flaws in him, including his lack of ambition. The Praetorian

Guard saw these weaknesses too, but these flaws were the reasons why they put him on the throne. They wanted a malleable figure who would secure their interests.

The Senate had long lost its claws, and it had no choice but to accept Claudius as the empire's legitimate ruler. Claudius had lived through the reigns of three emperors (he was four years old by the time his grand-uncle Augustus died), so he had seen the harsh reality of what happened when one donned the purple toga. Knowing both his reign and survival depended on the very people who had put him on the throne, Claudius rewarded the Praetorian Guard with substantial bribes, which earned him their loyalty. Gone were the days when emperors rose solely by their lineage or political support. The Praetorian Guard now had the power.

Decades after the assassination of Caligula, the Eternal City witnessed yet another deadly plot to remove its emperor. This time around, it was Nero, whose reign is infamously known for both extravagance and cruelty. Much like Caligula, Nero had a good start. He ruled the empire with promise, yet by 65 CE, his increasing paranoia, coupled with his wasteful spending on personal projects and persecution of political rivals, stirred deep resentment among the Romans, especially among the aristocrats. The art-obsessed emperor further eroded his support after the Great Fire of Rome in 64 CE. Rumor says that the fire was started by the emperor himself when he ordered a land clearance for the construction of his lavish palace known as the Domus Aurea ("Golden House"). Despite fires being common in Rome, this particular one ravaged the city for several days, destroying over half of it. Interestingly, Nero was not even in Rome when the fire broke out.

When the public began to point their fingers at the emperor, his reaction was to blame the Christians. Leveraging on the public's negative view of Christians, Nero accused them of being the culprits. He arrested, tortured, and brutally executed them. Tacitus recalled that the emperor ordered horrific punishments. While some Christians were torn by dogs, others were crucified in the Circus of Nero. They were burned alive and served as torches in the emperor's garden.

Eventually, the Romans had enough of the emperor's violent charades. Gaius Calpurnius Piso was a well-connected aristocrat who was respected by both the elites and commoners. Piso was known for his oratory skills. His home was a gathering spot for those who quietly wished for the return of the republican system. They often met to criticize Nero's brutal rule, but by 65 CE, their complaints had turned into a discussion of a plot. Joined by a group of senators, equestrians, and even the Praetorian Guard, the group planned on overthrowing Nero and putting Piso on top, as they believed he had the capabilities to restore order and respect to the empire.

Known as the Pisonian conspiracy, it involved some forty men, including Seneca, Nero's former tutor. Their strategy was rather straightforward. They were to assassinate the emperor during a public performance in the Circus Maximus and declare Piso the new ruler. Since they had the support of the Praetorian Guard, the plan was supposed to go smoothly. However, the conspiracy was foiled before it could even begin. One of the conspirators, Milichus, chose to betray the group. The freedman went to Nero's trusted advisor, Tigellinus, and revealed the details of the coup. As expected, Nero, who was already struggling with paranoia like his predecessors, acted hastily and brutally. A relentless purge was initiated across the Eternal City, targeting not only the conspirators but also anyone who was suspected of disloyalty. Piso and Seneca were forced to commit suicide.

The Great Fire of Rome.[22]

The conspiracy had failed terribly. Nero only grew more paranoid and was on guard day and night. As for the Senate, it was humiliated further since Nero's reign of terror resumed. Eventually, a series of political and military upheavals took place. Revolts plagued the empire, and Nero's royal bodyguards turned against him. Nero was eventually declared a public enemy by the very Senate he had constantly humiliated. When he finally had no other way out—even after fleeing Rome and hiding in one of his freedmen's villas—Nero stabbed himself in the throat.

Cicero, Whose Speeches and Words Cost Him His Own Life

Of course, emperors and dictators were not the only ones who became targets of assassination. Even senators had the possibility of meeting their demise in a brutal fashion. One such tragic figure was Marcus Tullius Cicero, who lived before Rome was made into an empire. Aside from being a member of the Senate, Cicero was also a skilled orator whose life was dedicated to defending the foundations of the Roman Republic.

Born in 106 BCE, Cicero had it all. He was born into a wealthy equestrian family. He was neither a soldier nor a war general; the senator was described by many to be a man of words, law, and politics. He was made a consul in 63 BCE and polished his reputation when he successfully thwarted the Catiline conspiracy. Cicero had a hand in saving the republic from internal revolts multiple times. So, it was not a surprise when Cicero pledged his support to Pompey the Great during Caesar's civil war.

Ever a man of politics, the senator sought reconciliation after Caesar gained victory, perhaps somehow believing that Rome could still be saved and its republican roots fully restored. However, everything changed when Caesar was assassinated. Power was quickly divided between a new set of leaders: Mark Antony, Octavian, and Lepidus. Mark Antony, in particular, was considered a threat to the Roman Republic, at least in the eyes of Cicero. He saw Antony as a corrupt and tyrannical figure. Antony's relationship with Cleopatra fueled Cicero to throw even more negative criticism at the general. With Caesar gone (Cicero knew he could not act when the dictator was alive since Antony was his closest friend and ally), Cicero was free to strike. He launched a series of speeches known as the *Philippics*, which were modeled after the orations of Demosthenes against Philip of Macedon. These speeches were thought of as a way to bring down Mark Antony. They labeled the general as a grave danger to Roman liberty and acted as a plea for the Senate to take a stand against him.

Some senators wasted no time in joining Cicero's cause. However, this success also signed his death warrant, as Antony began to plot his revenge. Cicero's life was threatened when the Second Triumvirate was formed. Mark Antony, Augustus (then Octavian), and Lepidus joined hands and drew up a proscription list, which contained the names of their enemies. These names were then marked for death, and their properties were seized. Antony insisted Cicero's name be included on the list. Octavian hesitated at first since Cicero had shown him support during the early years of his career. However, for the sake of maintaining the alliance with Mark Antony, he relented.

Soldiers under the order of Mark Antony dragged Cicero out of his litter.[23]

With the triumvirs aiming for his head, Cicero planned on fleeing Rome. He first sought refuge at his villa in Formia before leaving by sea. Unfortunately for the senator, Antony's soldiers tracked him down. Knowing that his time had come, legend has it that Cicero accepted his fate with calmness. He extended his neck and famously uttered, "There is nothing proper about what you are doing, but at least do it properly."

The severed head of Cicero, inspected by Fulvia, the wife of Mark Antony.[24]

Although Cicero's final act was one of dignity, his enemies were not planning to act the same. The soldiers severed his head and hands. These parts of Cicero were then taken back to the Eternal City, where they were nailed to the Rostra, a large platform, in the Roman Forum. Ironically, this was the very platform where Cicero had once delivered his speeches defending the Roman Republic and condemning tyranny. The sight of his severed body parts served as a vicious warning to others who dared to even think of opposing the Triumvirate.

Chapter 6 – The Cult of Mithras

Secret societies are not only limited to the modern world. They have existed for centuries. Their meetings and discussions were often cloaked in mystery and, most of the time, controversial intrigues. Secret rituals were common among the members of these kinds of societies, with each of them sworn to oaths and codes of conduct known only by their members. The purposes of these societies varied; some sought to protect a certain knowledge, others aimed to wield power, and some were spiritual in nature. The one thing they had in common was their need for secrecy, as they aimed to hide their true motives and actions from the larger world.

Today, many may be familiar with the Illuminati and the Knights Templar. Founded in Bavaria in 1776, the Illuminati was an intellectual movement aimed at promoting Enlightenment ideals and opposing religious and state control. However, as time went by, different views of society arose, many of which were based on conspiracy theories. Today, many claim that the members of the Illuminati are the ones who secretly control global political and economic systems.

The Knights Templar, on the other hand, was founded back in the 12th century. Created by a medieval order of warrior monks, its mission was to protect Christian pilgrims traveling to the Holy Land. The knights were also famous for their role in the Crusades.

These knights were known for their white mantles with a red cross and their strict vows of poverty, chastity, and obedience. They were involved in early banking activities (which made them one of the first organizations to provide financial services like loans and safekeeping), and they generated a fortune from donations made by kings and nobles. Their wealth and influence brought about their downfall.

In the 14th century, King Philip IV of France, who was said to be deeply in debt to the Templars, accused them of heresy. They were arrested, and their assets were seized. By 1312, the order had been disbanded, with some members subjected to execution. The order's sudden downfall soon led to various conspiracy theories. While some believe they had grown too powerful for the ruling class to tolerate, others thought they held secret knowledge or treasures like the Holy Grail or the Ark of the Covenant.

If we were to journey further back into time, when Zeus and Poseidon were still actively worshiped and the pyramids were still being constructed, we could find other secret societies. Both the Cult of Isis and the Cult of Dionysus played a big role in the religious and social life of the ancient world.

While the Cult of Isis originated in ancient Egypt and was established to worship the goddess of fertility and magic, Isis, the Cult of Dionysus was formed in ancient Greece. Popularly known as the god of wine, fertility, and ecstasy, Dionysus was worshiped differently compared to Isis. The cult's rites involved drinking, dancing, and revelry. Its rituals were designed to break down societal norms and constraints, allowing worshipers to experience a sense of freedom from the rigid structures of Greek society. Of course, these rites did not sit well with the authorities; they were seen as a potential source of social unrest. To avoid any mishap, the Cult of Dionysus operated in secret, with its members sworn to protect the mysteries of their worship.

In ancient times, it was normal for a secret society or cult to emerge from the worshiping of a certain god. The Cult of Mithras captured the imaginations of many in the 1st century CE. The cult was popular among the Roman military. The Cult of Mithras held the deity Mithras in high regard, though he was not openly worshiped in Roman temples like the gods of Olympus. In fact, Mithras was a figure of worship hidden from the public eye. Rituals involving the deity were practiced only by a select few.

Mithras originally belonged to the Persian pantheon, where he was acknowledged as a powerful divine being associated with light, truth, and the cosmic order. Being one of the central figures in the Zoroastrian religion, Mithras was also thought to be the mediator between the supreme god known as Ahura Mazda and humanity. As a guardian of cosmic balance, Mithras's task was to maintain justice and truth in the world. He was to oversee contracts and oaths while ensuring the forces of chaos and darkness were kept at bay.

Because of this, his worship among Persians centered around his role as the protector of the faithful and the god who upheld justice. His usual depiction was a solar deity riding a chariot across the sky, ensuring the sun would shine upon the earth. Of course, as time went by, the worship of Mithras transformed, especially when Persia's influence came into contact with other cultures beyond its borders.

The same could be said about the Roman Empire as it expanded its borders eastward. Although the Romans conquered many territories, bringing them under the empire's banner, they did not shy away from adapting new traditions and religious beliefs originating from these regions; the Cult of Mithras was definitely one of them. The worship of Mithras began with the Roman soldiers stationed in the eastern provinces (particularly those in modern-day Turkey and Syria). Perhaps impressed by the Persian god's warrior-like qualities and his associations with loyalty, truth, and victory over darkness, the Roman military found a sense of purpose in looking up to the divine being. After all, the soldiers were a long way from home and had been constantly facing the violent threat of war. Mithras offered them a sense of protection and strength.

When these Roman legions returned to the Eternal City after years of campaigning in the east, they brought along new religious ideas. Mithras became fully integrated into the Roman religion. Although most of the god's attributes remained, Mithras was not exactly the same as in Persian mythology. In Rome, Mithras was brought in as the god of soldiers. He was a symbol of discipline, loyalty, and victory. His role as a mediator was retained, though it took on a new significance in the Roman world; members of the Cult of Mithras saw themselves as part of a cosmic struggle between the forces of order and chaos.

Archaeological discoveries have revealed to us how far the Cult of Mithras flourished across the Roman Empire. One of the most significant discoveries was the Mithraeum, or temple dedicated to Mithras, found at Carrawburgh, a site along Hadrian's Wall in Britain. Hadrian's Wall was a Roman defensive fortification, and Carrawburgh was a military outpost. This underground temple, complete with an altar and reliefs of Mithras slaying a bull, shows that even soldiers stationed in far-off places, like the edges of the Roman Empire in Britain, practiced Mithraism. This was, of course, not just an ordinary bull. According to myth, the bull represents a primal cosmic creature whose death gave birth to life. When Mithras performed the sacrifice known as tauroctony, the bull's body and blood were believed to have generated new life—a ritual that symbolized the cycle of life, death, and rebirth.

The Mithraeum could also be found in the heart of the empire itself. Located in Rome under the Basilica of San Clemente, the Mithraeum was first rediscovered in the 19th century. Its intricate frescoes and carvings depicting the Persian god were still intact. This discovery confirmed the deep connection between the cult and elite Roman society. At the Roman port city Ostia, archaeologists discovered several temples dedicated to Mithras. Only one was well preserved, but it shed light on the activities held by the cult members. The temple featured stone benches arranged along the walls, which scholars believe were used for ritual feasts, a common activity held by those in cults.

The ruins of the Mithraeum in Ostia Antica, Italy.[25]

The Mithraea were unique. Unlike the grand temples of Jupiter, Mars, or Apollo that dotted the cities of the empire, Mithraea were typically smaller in size. Usually built within underground caves, it was common for the temples to be only dimly lit. This subterranean setting was not just for the sake of design. It was symbolic of the hidden nature of the cult and represented the journey from darkness to light. The cave-like atmosphere was also thought to be a reflection of the mythological setting where Mithras slayed the sacred bull. Although the Mithraea were not as spacious as the grand temples of Rome—they could hold only a few dozen members at the same time—the spaces were more intimate, allowing a tight-knit brotherhood to be formed among the initiates.

Each Mithraeum featured a centerpiece, an image of Mithras slaying the bull. The deity could be seen posing heroically as he thrust a dagger into the neck of a mighty bull. This scene was accompanied by various other animals, including a dog, a snake, and a scorpion. Scholars believe that this iconography also represented the cosmic struggle between life and death and light and darkness. The bull's blood, in Mithraic belief, was thought to bring fertility and renewal, while the act of sacrifice symbolized the victory of order over chaos. For members of the cult, the image was a reminder of their role in this cosmic battle and that they had aligned themselves with the forces of light, represented by Mithras.

The cult bore several similarities to other secret societies in our modern world; its appeal lay in its exclusivity and secrecy. Those who chose to be a part of its mysteries were bound together in brotherhood, with Mithras acknowledged as their divine leader. Perhaps it was this very sense of camaraderie that attracted many soldiers of the empire to take a vow and become initiated into the cult.

Not every soul could gain entry into the Cult of Mithras. Its teachings, rites, and rituals were held in secret, known only to initiates who had undergone a series of complex and symbolic initiation rites. These rites were not just a requirement for entry; they were designed to test both the physical and spiritual strength of the initiate so that they could further prepare themselves on a deeper journey to understanding the cosmic mysteries associated with Mithras.

To enter the cult, initiates had to pass through seven levels of initiation. Each of these levels represented a higher state of spiritual understanding and connection to Mithras. Apart from being symbolic, these stages were also practical, as they each carried specific duties and responsibilities. The first level of initiation was known as Corax (Raven). The lowest rank among all seven, Corax was associated with the element of air. Initiates at this stage were symbolically connected to the raven, a bird that served Mithras and carried messages. This was also when an initiate would take oaths of loyalty to the cult and to Mithras himself; it was the very beginning of their spiritual journey.

The second level was Nymphus (Bridegroom), which was associated with water, which symbolized purity and transformation. At this level, initiates would take on the role of a bridegroom and be metaphorically wedded to Mithras. This represented a bond or commitment to the faith. The third initiation level was Miles. Those at this level were considered soldiers of Mithras, emphasizing the militaristic nature of the cult. Initiates had to portray courage and dedication in battle in Mithras's service.

The fourth level was named Leo. Associated with fire and the image of a lion, this level marked a significant advancement in the cult. Initiates who reached this level were considered guardians of the Mithraeum, and their main responsibility was to maintain the sacred space. Once they passed this level, the initiates would go to the fifth level, Perses. Named after the Persian origin of Mithras, this level symbolized spiritual wisdom. Initiates were seen as intermediaries between the earthly and divine realms. They were almost like Mithras himself.

The sixth level of initiation was named Heliodromus or the "Sun-Runner." Just as its name suggested, this level was associated with the sun, the symbol of ultimate light and truth. Those who had come all this way and reached this rank were considered to have attained a close connection to Mithras. Last but not least, the highest rank of all was Pater ("Father"), which was reserved only for the elders and leaders of the secret cult. As the "Father," those in this rank were the spiritual guides or teachers responsible for leading rituals and the initiation of new members. They were also seen as fully integrated into the cosmic mysteries of Mithras.

Much like the depiction of the tauroctony (where Mithras slayed the bull), initiation ceremonies often mimicked the struggle between life and death. The most essential part of the Mithraic practice was the communal meals, which mirrored the brotherhood of the Roman army. Bread and wine were consumed by members of the cult, and they could have been symbols of the sacred bull's flesh and blood. Apart from being a ritualistic practice, this act was also a way to strengthen bonds between initiates, creating a sense of loyalty that greatly defined the Mithraic brotherhood.

A relief showing a depiction of the tauroctony found near Heidelberg.[26]

The Mithraic mysteries also had a strong astrological connection. The depiction of the tauroctony alone was believed to have been more than just a sacrificial image. Many agreed that it might have had astrological connotations. The bull, for instance, was thought to represent the zodiac sign Taurus. Meanwhile, the scorpion could be identified with the zodiac sign Scorpio. Its depiction of stinging the bull's genitals could symbolize Scorpio's position opposite Taurus in the zodiac. Its act of attacking the bull might also be a symbol of cosmic struggle. While the image of the dog leaping up at the bull's wound might not be directly linked to a specific zodiac sign, scholars agree that it might represent the constellation Canis Major or Canis Minor.

As for the snake, which could be seen near the bull and, at times, depicted drinking its blood, its image could be linked to the constellation Hydra, though its specific astrological role remains debated. The raven, which at times appeared perched near Mithras, represents the constellation Corvus, the messenger between gods and humans.

Of course, like many other mystery cults of the ancient world, the influence of the Cult of Mithras began to wane as time passed by. When

Christianity rose under Emperor Constantine and officially turned into a state religion by Emperor Theodosius I in 380 CE, Mithraism and many other pagan beliefs were suppressed. The cult's exclusivity and secretive nature contributed greatly to its decline. While Christianity sought to convert the masses and offered salvation to all, Mithraism was only open to a select group of men, particularly soldiers and the elites. When Christianity spread across the edges of the empire, carrying a universal message of salvation and eternal life, the mysterious cult struggled to maintain its foothold.

With Christianity becoming the official religion of the empire, the Romans saw an increasing number of decrees outlawing pagan practices. Churches and basilicas began to be constructed to replace temples. While some were repurposed and converted into churches, the Mithraea were left abandoned or destroyed. The cult's decline was indeed rapid. Mithraism disappeared from public life just as the curtains were about to close on the 4th century CE.

What is left for us today is only questions. Unlike Christianity, which left behind scriptures, letters, and early theological works for us to dissect, Mithraism left little to no written doctrine. The teachings and rituals of the cult were likely passed down orally from initiator to initiates. They were never recorded in a way that could survive the test of time, or if they were any, it could be plausible that they were purposely destroyed. The remains of the Mithraea, the relics and images of the tauroctony, and a few surviving inscriptions are the only ways we can get a glimpse into the religious practices of the cult. Much of its inner workings are forever lost, making them a true untold story.

Chapter 7 – The Roman Entertainment: Gladiatorial Games and Chariot Races

Excitement filled the air as the citizens of Rome made their way into the Colosseum. They were eager to see a certain figure: Carpophorus, the legendary *bestiarius* who had already cemented his name in the history of Rome for his mastery of the deadly art of combat against beasts.

Carpophorus was far from an ordinary *bestiarius*. Typically, *bestiarii* were either criminals or prisoners of war thrown into the arena to fight wild animals as punishment. It is safe to assume that most *bestiarii* were condemned to death. Many often resorted to suicide rather than face their demise in the jaws and claws of a lion or bear. Carpophorus took his fate as a challenge. He rose above the expectations and slew some of the most ferocious beasts ever brought to Rome. He turned these battles into spectacles of strength and cunning, leading to the cheers of the blood-loving Romans.

Some even believed Carpophorus possessed a supernatural ability to read the minds of these beasts. They claimed that he was able to predict every move of the creatures with ultimate precision. Others suggested that he was favored by the gods, who generously gifted him with otherworldly strength.

The time had finally come. The heavy iron gate creaked open, and loud cheering soon burst out when the audience saw Carpophorus stepping into the arena. He was a sight to behold. Like the seasoned gladiators, Carpophorus was muscular yet lean, and his body showed marks created by years of combat. His armor was minimal. It was designed not for protection but for speed and agility. He only had a spear in his hands, its tip sharp enough to pierce through even the toughest of hides.

A 5ᵗʰ-century mosaic in the Great Palace of Constantinople picturing a fight against a tiger.[37]

The first beast was unleashed. It was a lion, his golden mane suggesting that it was mature enough to lead a pride. The crowds hushed and leaned forward, wondering if this was the last time they would ever see Carpophorus in action, though it was unlikely since the *bestiarius* had slain many lions before. After a few moments of scanning the arena, the lion let out a roar and charged forward. This did not shatter Carpophorus's resolve; he held his ground and waited for the right opportunity. When the lion was inches away from him, the *bestiarius* quickly sidestepped the beast, avoiding its giant claw of death. Then, with a single, powerful thrust, Carpophorus drove his spear deep into the lion's side. The creature's roar turned into a weak growl before the lion collapsed to the ground.

The crowd stood and cheered for the talented *bestiarius*, yet Carpophorus remained calm. This was just the beginning of the day. Legend has it that there was a time when the *bestiarius* fought relentlessly against twenty wild beasts in a single day.

A bear was released into the arena. It rose onto its hind legs and towered over the muscular Carpophorus. The *bestiarius* circled the beast and read the animal's movements. When the bear swiped its massive paw, Carpophorus ducked. Noticing an opening, he drove his spear into the bear's exposed chest.

At this point in time, the crowds were chanting his name. More beasts were unleashed. Next was a tiger, its stripes striking and jaws deadly. Then came a hulking rhinoceros, its every footstep making the ground tremble. Afterward, a group of hyenas came running out, their snapping jaws attempting to end the Carpophorus's life. Last but not least, a wild boar charged forward with unrelenting fury. Carpophorus successfully put an end to each one, and when the last beast fell, he raised his spear in triumph.

But, of course, beneath the glory of the arena lay the harsh reality of a gladiator's life. Fighters like Carpophorus were not always born into fame and opportunity. The majority of them had rather difficult beginnings. They were prisoners of war, criminals, or even slaves whose careers in the arena were actually a form of punishment. This was not always the case, though. There were those who joined the arena willingly so they could get their hands on wealth to escape a life of poverty. Regardless of the reasons, all of the gladiators were subjected to relentless training before their names were called to enter the violent contests.

Gladiators were divided into multiple classes, and each of them was defined by its equipment and fighting styles. The *retiarius* fought with a trident and a net, which he used to ensnare his opponents, and the *secutores* were best known for their helmets with small eye slits, heavy shields, and short swords used for close combat. The heavily armored *murmillo* usually wore fish-shaped helmets, while the *Thraex* were armed in the Thracian style. They carried curved swords and a *parmula* (a small shield) and were lightly armored. Each class had its own strengths and weaknesses, allowing game hosts to orchestrate a balanced match to enthrall spectators.

A 2ⁿᵈ-century CE mosaic depicting gladiators.[28]

The *bestiarii*, like Carpophorus, were unique among the gladiators. Instead of going against other men, they fought wild beasts brought into the Eternal City from lands far away; this included lions, bears, bulls, and other exotic animals to the Romans, such as leopards and rhinoceroses. The *bestiarii* were, more often than not, supplied with minimal armor compared to the typical gladiators. This was so that they could fully utilize their speed and precision rather than their brute strength. Carpophorus usually favored fighting primarily with a spear and, at times, a dagger.

Interestingly, historical records suggest the *bestiarii* were often of African origin. This conclusion was made due to the fact that Rome had brought in a large number of slaves from North Africa. The Africans were also thought to have possessed a unique understanding of wild animals, especially those native to their homelands. However, this remains a topic of debate; even Carpophorus's origin is a mystery to us.

Although the arenas were mostly dominated by male gladiators, historical accounts suggest that female gladiators existed, though they were not as common. Known as gladiatrices, they were considered a novelty, and their participation in fights was meant to add excitement for the spectators. These women who chose a life in the arena were thought to have made the decision willingly; they were either motivated by a desire for independence or financial rewards. Although it seems a woman gave up any claim to respectability as soon as she entered the arena, there is some evidence to suggest that female gladiators were honored as highly as their male counterparts.

Perhaps one of the misconceptions about gladiatorial combat was the idea that every fight ended with a single gladiator standing. This misconception was made popular by modern films. While some matches—especially the ones where the fighters were condemned criminals or hated individuals—were to the death, the majority of them were not. Owning gladiators was expensive. They had to be fed, trained, and housed. Losing a gladiator in every game meant losing an investment. Unless a fight was specifically designed to be a punishment, many fights ended with more than one gladiator surviving. A match did not have to end when blood was shed. Some ended when one gladiator was too injured to continue. Once this happened, the editor, the sponsor of the games, or even the roaring crowds could decide the loser's fate. Nevertheless, death in the arena was far less common than Hollywood has led many to believe.

A depiction of a gladiatorial fight (with audiences giving their thumbs down), painted in 1872.[19]

Gladiators who managed to earn a reputation were rewarded immensely. They were showered with prizes and wealth, but the most precious of all was an offer for freedom. Some gladiators were allowed to hang their weapons and never worry again about their fates in the arena.

A gladiator named Flamma was one of the fighters offered this chance. Originating from Syria, Flamma was a prisoner of war who successfully earned renown through victories in the arena. He was believed to have participated in thirty-four fights; he won twenty-one, drew nine, and lost only four matches—a feat very few could claim. Flamma was a crowd favorite. As he built his reputation, he was granted a golden chance to break free from the chains of servitude.

He was offered the wooden *rudis* more than once. The *rudis* was a public acknowledgment that the gladiator had earned his place among the free citizens of Rome. However, to the shock of many, he refused his freedom, turning down the *rudis* time and again. Many were puzzled by his decision, but perhaps Flamma had become fond of the Colosseum and the roar of the crowd. Perhaps the honor of combat outweighed the peace and freedom offered to him. The arena had become both his life and identity; stepping away from it meant he was abandoning the very thing that made him legendary.

The Colosseum was not the only place where Romans—regardless of their status in the hierarchy—flocked in search of entertainment. The elites, the plebeians (commoners), and even slaves sought blood-pumping spectacles at the Circus Maximus, where chariot races were held. The roots of chariot racing trace back to the Etruscans and Greeks, and it became a favorite pastime for the ancient Romans. Similar to the gladiators, charioteers were also made up of either prisoners of war, slaves, or those from humble or unfortunate backgrounds.

The Circus Maximus could house up to 150,000 people. Known to be the largest and most famous venue, the Circus Maximus featured an oval-shaped track on which charioteers would race each other at breakneck speeds. There were different teams in the race, which were often sponsored by wealthy elites. Divided into four factions (Red, Blue, Green, and White), each of them had their own loyal fans who would, at times, get involved in violent outbursts in the stands.

A model of the Circus Maximus (left) in the 4ᵗʰ century CE, along with the Colosseum in the far right.[30]

Since speed was key, the chariots were lightweight and not designed for protection. They were pulled by two, four, or even six horses. The charioteers had to steer their horses at high speeds while maintaining their balance during the sharp turns. This was not the only danger the racers had to face, as they were allowed to use violence in their bid for victory. Some would use their whips not only to lash their horses but also to strike a blow to their opponents. This attack would knock their opponents off balance and send them crashing, especially at the sharp turns of the track, where things could quickly turn deadly.

The charioteers had to complete all seven laps around the two-thousand-foot sand track. Reaching a top speed of nearly forty miles per hour, the charioteers had to stay vigilant at all times; even the smallest mistake could lead to a disastrous crash that could possibly claim their lives. The final stretch was where the brutal struggle between the racers reached its peak, as they would do everything in their power to ensure victory was theirs.

One of the most renowned charioteers was Gaius Appuleius Diocles. Born in the province of Lusitania (modern-day Portugal), Gaius began his career at the age of eighteen, racing for the White faction. By the time he reached 25, Gaius was said to have participated in over 4,200 races. Despite the dangerous nature of the sport, Gaius won 1,462 races, forever immortalizing his name as one of the greatest charioteers in Roman history. His victories undoubtedly rewarded him with immense wealth, with some sources claiming that he reportedly owned a fortune equivalent to millions in today's currency. He was named one of the richest athletes in the ancient world.

A modern depiction of a chariot race held in the Circus Maximus.[31]

A typical race involving Gaius Appuleius Diocles would have been a show of speed, violence, and danger. Before every race, the chariots lined up at the starting gates. Tension was probably high during this moment for both the racers and the audience. With a blast of the starting horn, the gates would fly open, giving way for the horses to gallop, leading the chariots forward. Dust would fill the air as the chariots skid around the curved track. As for Gaius, who had substantial experience, the sharp turns were no longer a challenge.

However, the race was not only about speed; survival was also of the utmost importance. Gaius aimed to tangle his closest opponent's reins, hoping it would send the chariot into a vicious crash at the sharp turn known as the *metae*. Collisions were common, and they were almost always followed by the cheers of spectators.

Betting was also a common sight among the spectators, with fortunes won and lost based on the outcome. Those who were desperate to tip the scales in their favor even went to the extent of relying on supernatural means. Archaeological findings of curse tablets found near Roman race tracks suggest that the spectators believed in divine intervention; these curses were usually written to harm racers from rival factions.

Gaius knew exactly when to pull the reins and to balance the aggression with caution. When he arrived first on the finishing line, his victory would be announced with a blast of a trumpet. Gaius would then be escorted to the judges' box, where he was presented with a wreath, a palm branch, and a prize in the form of money. Afterward, he would return to his chariot and take a quick lap around the track before the next race began.

Gaius Appuleius Diocles survived the race track for twenty-four years, yet not everyone could share his luck. Another famous figure on the track who went by the name Scorpus gained public recognition, yet his demise happened too soon.

Similar to Gaius, Scorpus achieved substantial success in the Circus Maximus, granting him both fame and wealth. Born as a slave, Scorpus raced for the Green faction and quickly became a fan favorite after the crowd witnessed his incredible speed and tactical skill on the track. He was highly talented, especially when it came to daring maneuvers. His quick reflexes also spared him from crashes—at least for a while—while his fearless approach around the *metae* made him a formidable opponent. Throughout his career as a charioteer, Scorpus won over two thousand races.

Unfortunately, his career was cut short when a tragedy struck him on the very track he had built his reputation on. Despite being known for his reflexes and skills at maneuvering the horses, Scorpus was killed in a collision at the *metae*. Many agreed that he died before his time. Scorpus was likely in his twenties when the crash took his life, a stark contrast to Gaius, who lived well into his forties. Although both men successfully achieved legendary status, Scorpus's early death proved the dangers of racing, as it only took a minor misstep before the gods could snatch away their lives. The young charioteer's passing affected his fans tremendously. They mourned the loss of a man who had once seemed invincible on the dusty track.

The Romans enjoyed these brutal forms of entertainment, yet when Christianity rose later on, the Roman Empire began to change its views on both gladiatorial games and chariot races. Seen as nothing more than barbaric, both games were banned by the end of the 4th century CE.

Chapter 8 – The Poisoned Emperors of Rome

Caligula's paranoia had turned into reality. He could only widen his eyes to express his disbelief. He wished to speak once more, yet not a word left his lips. It was all too late—the daggers had pierced his flesh, giving way for his thick blood to flow, staining the ground. The emperor had finally collapsed; Rome's most despised tyrant had been killed in cold blood.

News of Caligula's sudden death soon spread across the palace, resulting in more chaos in the Eternal City. The Senate had mixed feelings about the tyrant's death. The senators saw this as an opportunity to restore the republic, but the Praetorian Guard stood before them; they had other plans in mind. In one of the palace's chambers, the royal guards stumbled upon Claudius, the awkward and stuttering uncle of the dead emperor. He had seen it all, but fearing the same fate, Claudius hid himself behind a curtain. Much to his terror, the Praetorian Guard dragged him out. But instead of putting a sword to his throat, the royal guards hailed him as the new emperor—a decision that shocked many.

The Praetorian Guard proclaiming Claudius as the new emperor of Rome.[32]

Claudius was never on the list to run for emperor. Despite being the paternal uncle of Caligula, their relationship was complex and tense. He was a member of the imperial family, yet his reputation was nearly nonexistent, largely due to his perceived frailty and awkward demeanor. Claudius was initially treated fairly by his nephew when he first rose to the throne. He even held minor positions under Caligula, although they were mostly ceremonial, but as the young emperor's reign progressed, his deteriorating mental state began to corrupt him.

The very moment Caligula descended into madness, he became tremendously suspicious of those around him. He saw them as his enemies or even conspirators planning his murder. The early days of promise soon gave way to multiple episodes of cruelty and paranoia. Even Claudius was not free from Caligula's suspicions. Although Claudius never posed a threat to the throne, he was still a member of the imperial family. In Caligula's paranoid mind, Claudius could easily shift his support and turn into a potential rival.

According to the historian Suetonius, the emperor took pleasure in embarrassing him, often ridiculing his physical condition. Claudius was essentially turned into a jester before the Senate and the public, further reinforcing the idea that he was unfit to lead. At times, Claudius was even forced to participate in public spectacles where he was made to play the fool at banquets and feasts. Caligula also once jokingly auctioned off Claudius's wealth to embarrass his uncle.

Nonetheless, Claudius managed to survive his nephew's reign. Wanting to maintain a low profile, Claudius often relented to the emperor's orders, no matter how ridiculous they were. He endured the humiliation in silence and avoided displaying any political ambition. However, Caligula's paranoia knew no boundaries; although Claudius remained submissive, the emperor never stopped making threats, even toward his closest family members.

By the time Caligula breathed his last, Claudius had long since become disillusioned with his nephew. There is no direct evidence that shows Claudius's involvement in the assassination of Caligula. Although it could be plausible that he was at least aware of the growing discontent, especially among the Praetorian Guard and the Senate, Claudius likely kept his distance. He avoided getting involved in conspiracies, knowing that it might cost him his own life.

Whether or not he was actually informed about the plot, we can be sure that Claudius's life took a different turn the moment Caligula's lifeless body hit the marble ground. The Praetorian Guard saw him as a figure they could easily manipulate, which was why a wreath was handed to Claudius.

Rome was already unstable when Claudius sat on the throne. However, despite being known for his disabilities, Claudius showed a willingness to rebuild the empire. He knew the importance of the very people who had placed him on the throne. Thus, one of his first moves to secure his power was to reward both the Praetorian Guard and the military. He spoiled the Praetorians with a large *donativum* (a gift of money) to ensure he had their loyalty and allegiance. He also made generous grants to the Roman legions, pleasing them as a result. Although not exactly groomed to rule, Claudius was aware of the most important lesson as a ruler: in a time of turmoil, the person who controls the army controls the entire empire.

Claudius also paid attention to Rome's public infrastructure, which had long needed improvement. He continued the construction of two major aqueducts—named Aqua Claudia and Aqua Anio Novus—which had been started by his nephew. Completed in 52 CE, these structures drastically improved the water supply for Rome. Along with two other aqueducts (Aqua Anio Vetus and Aqua Marcia, which were commissioned in 272 BCE and 144 BCE, respectively), they became known as the four great aqueducts of Rome.

Aqua Claudia.[33]

Claudius undoubtedly surprised many with his capabilities to bring Rome back to its glory, albeit for a while. Understanding the importance of trade and grain supply, the emperor made the decision to expand the harbor at Ostia. This way, Rome was able to have a reliable supply of food at all times. Claudius also paid attention to improving the roads that connected the city with distant provinces. Because of this grand construction project, the military could respond to threats more efficiently. Claudius also took a personal interest in handling matters on the administrative front. He was involved in the judicial process, often presiding over cases himself.

The Roman bureaucracy improved when Claudius took the mantle. Through his legal reforms, the emperor was able to streamline governance and reduce corruption. Another major decision he made was to open bureaucratic positions to freedmen (former slaves who had been granted freedom). These men, perhaps appreciating his move not to favor only the aristocrats, were loyal to him.

The emperor was also said to have increased women's privileges and often displayed humility whenever he was with his subjects. Once, the emperor apologized to visiting pensioners after finding out there were not enough chairs prepared for them. This was the kind of behavior that, according to Suetonius, made the public love their emperor.

The most defining act of Claudius's reign came in the form of military conquests. The emperor launched the invasion of Britain in 43 CE, which resulted in the expansion of the empire's borders. New wealth was obtained from these campaigns, and the emperor solidified his rule. Claudius wished to stay away from the same mistakes his predecessors had made.

Unfortunately, no matter his efforts, the gods had already decided his fate; Claudius could not escape the brutality of politics. However, unlike Caligula or even Julius Caesar, Claudius would be a victim, not of the blade but of poison.

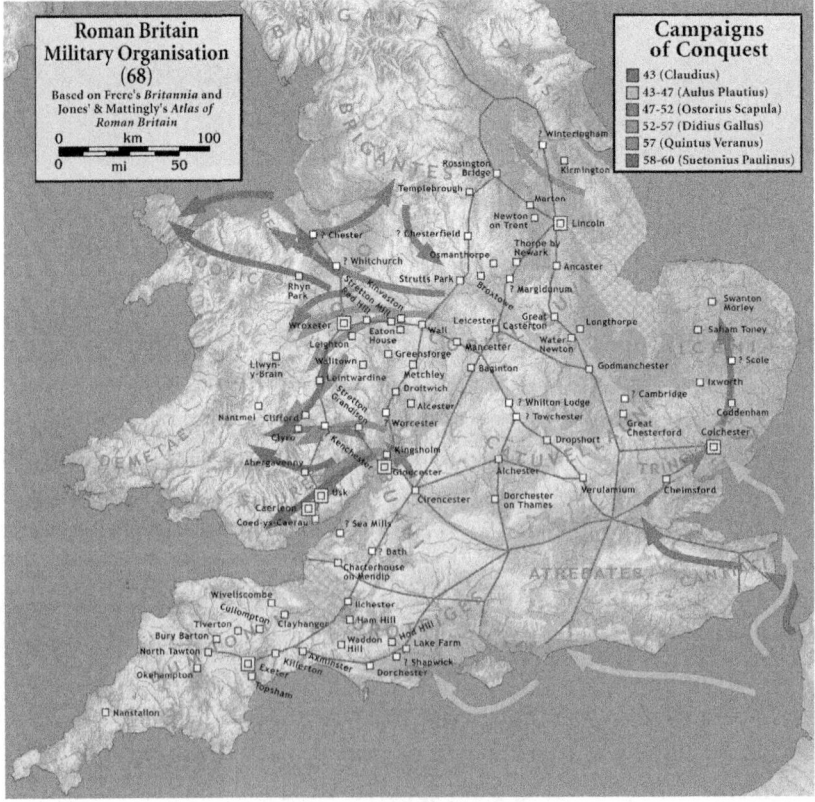

Roman conquest of Britain.[34]

Poisoning was—and still is—considered a popular method of eliminating people of power. Its subtlety made it a preferred tool for those seeking power without the risk of public spectacle. Compared to daggers, which left obvious evidence of murder, poison allowed the assassin to remove their targets in a quieter and more calculated way. During a time when forensics was not yet advanced, the cause of death could often be wrongly concluded. The dead could be thought to have died from natural causes while the real culprit was actually poison. Suspicions would, of course, linger, especially if it was a sudden death, yet without concrete proof, nothing could be done.

As for Claudius, his greatest weakness was, ironically, his trust in others. Despite being a capable ruler, Claudius tended to misplace his trust. His greatest enemy turned out to be none other than his wives, first Messalina and later Agrippina the Younger (who was also his niece).

Agrippina had one ambition: to secure the throne for her son, Nero. When Claudius's health worsened and his performance in governing the empire began to see the first few signs of deterioration, Agrippina made a move. Instead of using sharp weapons to eliminate the emperor, she chose poison, hoping it could mimic natural causes. Of course, Agrippina did not plan on removing Claudius all by herself. She had the help of those closest to the emperor, particularly the servants, advisors, and the freedmen-turned-officials whom Claudius had appointed years ago. The plan was to serve the emperor a dish of mushrooms—said to be his favorite food—with poison injected in them. It was also widely believed that the poison was created by Locusta of Gaul, a notorious poisoner and possibly the first serial killer in history.

Unsuspecting of the plot, Claudius devoured the mushrooms, only to fall ill afterward. However, the emperor did not die. Agrippina was quick to administer a second dose of poison, possibly through a feather that was used on the emperor to induce vomiting. The emperor finally met his demise. It was ruled that Claudius had died of illness. Because of this, Agrippina successfully avoided suspicion, though whispers of the emperor being murdered followed her.

Despite Claudius's tragic ending, the emperor's name was not listed in the same category as his nephew. He was able to maintain a reputation as a competent ruler, even though he was once the black sheep of his family.

Yet, years after Claudius, Rome would again be thrown into a period of chaos when a new emperor rose to the throne. Named Commodus, the emperor would be forever known as the worst tyrant to ever hold the throne.

Commodus came to power in a very different Rome from the one Claudius knew. By the time he rose as emperor, the Roman Empire had endured different episodes of crisis, including a brief experiment with co-emperors. This system was initially established as an attempt to share the burdens of leadership. After all, Rome had transformed into a sprawling empire that stretched from Britain to the Near East. However, this system of co-rulership did not curb the issues that the empire was struggling with. Competition for power only intensified, leading the Eternal City to enter another state of political unrest. It was not until the rise of the philosopher-emperor Marcus Aurelius in 161 CE that the empire finally got its taste of stability once again.

Marcus Aurelius's reign, in many ways, represented the height of Roman virtue. Apart from his Stoic philosophy, the emperor was also a man of ultimate discipline. He was best known for his strategic governance. Although Rome faced constant wars on its borders and battled a plague that shook the city, Marcus Aurelius never faltered. Being one of the Five Good Emperors, Marcus Aurelius ruled over the empire and watched it flourish for nearly two decades. His only decision that would haunt the empire for years to come was when he appointed his son, the fifteen-year-old Commodus, as co-emperor in 177 CE (three years prior to his death).

It did not take long for the Romans to notice that Commodus was the complete opposite of his father. While Marcus Aurelius was often praised for being thoughtful and disciplined, Commodus was impulsive, cruel, and indulgent. The historian Aelius Lampridius later described the young emperor with words such as dishonorable and lewd—he even claimed Commodus to be defiled of mouth and debauched. Other historians agree that although Rome had suffered under the reign of emperors like Caligula and Nero, at least they began their reigns with promise. With Commodus, however, terror could be seen the very moment he first sat on the throne.

Commodus officially took over the reins in 180 CE when Marcus Aurelius died. He inherited an empire that was relatively stable, largely thanks to his father. Yet, the young emperor had little, if any, interest in governance. He only had his eyes on the luxury and privileges of wearing the purple toga rather than the burden of leadership. Instead of handling state matters in person, Commodus delegated the day-to-day tasks to several of his most trusted lieutenants. However, just like his predecessors, Commodus developed trust issues. Whenever he smelled even the slightest scent of disobedience, he would turn against his lieutenants. Even without securing concrete evidence, the emperor would have them murdered and find another person to fill the position.

Commodus did not pay much attention to governing the vast empire, yet it was clear that he enjoyed its spoils. As an emperor, the immense wealth of Rome was at his disposal, and he never hesitated to use it to pursue his own desires. Commodus was especially passionate about the gladiatorial games. However, unlike most emperors who enjoyed the games from the imperial box, Commodus took a more active role in the arena. While his father was well known on the battlefield (Marcus Aurelius spent much of his reign leading Roman armies in the Marcomannic Wars), Commodus only showed his teeth fighting against gladiators and beasts, though most of the combat was staged. The historian Cassius Dio once noted that Commodus boasted that he personally slayed a hundred lions in a single day.

Commodus's participation in the gladiatorial games.[85]

The arena was also where he displayed his cruelty. In one particular spectacle, the young emperor brought out a group of men, all of whom had lost their feet, and dressed them as serpents. Armed with sponges instead of rocks, these people had to pretend they were giants attacking the emperor. Perhaps playing the hero, Commodus clubbed them to death. Nevertheless, despite enjoying these violent performances, Commodus toned down his excitement whenever he was going against actual gladiators. Although there were records suggesting that the emperor did kill men in the arena, historians debate whether or not his victims were real fighters. Since the spectacles were usually manipulated to save the emperor from embarrassment, many suspected his opponents were not skilled gladiators but people forced into combat.

As his reign continued, his delusions grew more pronounced. Commodus was infamously obsessed with Hercules, the god of strength. He even went as far as to claim that he was the reincarnation of the god. In an attempt to convince his subjects of his claim, the young emperor could often be seen dressed in a lion-skin cloak and, at times, wielding a club. He spent an enormous amount of money building statues of him as the demi-god and hosting festivals. The statues of Nero were demolished to be replaced with ones of Commodus dressed as Hercules.

It is not surprising that Commodus was described as a narcissist. He once attempted to rename the months of the calendar so they would all be his name. This was a tradition that had been briefly adopted by earlier Roman leaders. July, for example, was named after Julius Caesar, and August was named after Augustus. However, most Romans refused to acknowledge the changes that Commodus made. He further displayed his narcissistic side when a massive fire engulfed parts of the Eternal City in 191. Instead of leading the recovery efforts, the emperor's contribution was to rename the city Colonia Lucia Annia Commodiana,

A statue of Commodus as Hercules.[86]

which translates to Commodus's Colony. He then announced his decree that required his subjects to be referred to as Commodiani, and the Roman Senate was rebranded the Commodian Fortunate Senate.

The young emperor's erratic behavior undoubtedly alienated much of the Roman aristocracy. Multiple assassination attempts were hatched, though they all failed. One of the major attempts happened in 182. Instigated by his own sister, Lucilla, who was furious with the emperor's excesses, the plot involved several senators. The plan was to perhaps recreate the assassination of Julius Caesar, as the conspirators were to stab the emperor with a dagger. Unfortunately, one of the conspirators had cold feet at the last minute. Commodus survived, and Lucilla was exiled and executed later on.

The second attempt took place in 187, but it resulted in a harsh purge. Instead of ridding Rome of the cruel emperor, the foiled assassination conspiracy led to the murder of dozens of senators. Another attempt was made in 192, and this one was almost a success. By this point in time, Commodus had distanced himself from almost everyone in power. The coup was spearheaded by two of his most trusted high-ranking officials, Laetus and Eclectus. After securing an allegiance with the emperor's mistress, Marcia, the conspirators made haste to save the empire before Commodus could do more harm.

Poison was their first weapon of choice. They slipped a lethal dose into his wine or beef. Yet, the emperor managed to vomit out the meal, so the poison failed to kill him. Not planning on letting the plan fail, the conspirators turned to Narcissus, a professional wrestler, to finish the job. Commodus, now weakened by the poison, was resting in his chamber when Narcissus entered. The wrestler strangled the emperor to death.

And so, Rome was finally free from its luxury-loving emperor, the one who thought of himself as Hercules reborn. He died at the age of thirty-one, and his departure marked the end of the Antonine dynasty.

Chapter 9 – Smugglers, Pirates, and Underground Markets

A merchant ship could be seen calmly entering the bustling port of Ostia. There was nothing special about its cargo–just another set of crates filled with pottery. The crew moved quickly, unloading the goods under the watchful eyes of the Roman customs officials. It all looked normal, but the crew could feel their hearts beating faster than usual. Apart from the pottery, which looked like they were destined for the market, the merchant ship also secretly carried sacks of Egyptian grain, olive oil, and even spices that they had not declared. They knew the risks of smuggling, but they were more attracted to the rewards.

The ruins of a marketplace in Ostia, where merchants from across continents flocked to.[37]

The Eternal City was popularly known for its tariffs and taxes. Goods flowed in from distant provinces like Egypt, Hispania, and Syria, but these goods were heavily taxed, making certain imports almost prohibitively expensive. Grain from Egypt, for instance, was taxed heavily after the region was annexed by the empire. Other valuable goods coming from the East, including olive oil and exotic spices, were also targets for high taxation. The Roman government relied on its ports and taxes to fill its treasury. Yet, for the merchants, the heavy taxes were burdensome. They found the allure of avoiding taxes too great to resist.

This was where smugglers came into the picture. Those who chose this as a career were not typical criminals who lurked in dark alleys. Instead, they were often seasoned traders who understood the Roman trading system. To become a smuggler, one needed to master two main skills: forging shipping documents and disguising valuable goods as everyday items. Another skill was to have a keen eye; smugglers had to look for port officials who might abandon the law for the sake of money.

Smugglers had to keep a careful eye on their rivals. Perhaps hoping to gain favor with the authorities, they might tip off Roman officials and ruin the plan entirely. Once smuggling activity was discovered, punishment was swift. Although the punishment varied depending on the nature of the crime, the status of the person involved, and the goods being smuggled, the most common punishments were fines, the confiscation of goods, and imprisonment, especially for repeat offenders. Execution was reserved for more severe cases, especially for those who smuggled items seen as an affront to state security. This included military goods, weapons, and other contraband that could be used to undermine Rome's stability.

Despite the serious punishments, the underground trade network continued to flourish. The elites depended on a steady supply of luxury goods, and the official markets could not always meet the demand. The grain shortage in 22 CE, for instance, brought fortune to smugglers. The wealthy Romans were able to continue hosting banquets and feed their households because of smugglers. The commoners might have cursed the shortages and the spike in prices due to scarcity, but the elites were never hungry, thanks to the underground economy.

The most famous episode of smuggling came in the 6th century CE when the empire was already split into two halves: the Western Roman Empire and the Eastern Roman Empire (better known as the Byzantine Empire). During this period of time, silk was considered one of the most valuable materials in the world, but the secret of producing it was guarded by China. The only way to import it was through the Silk Road, making silk extremely expensive and difficult to obtain.

When two Christian monks who had traveled to China finally learned of the process of making silk, Emperor Justinian I ordered them to smuggle silkworm eggs back to the Byzantine Empire. The silkworm eggs were hidden inside hollow bamboo canes and safely brought to Constantinople, allowing the Byzantines to produce their own silk. This broke China's monopoly and benefitted the Roman Empire tremendously.

Other than food supplies and luxury items, the smuggling networks in Rome also extended to one of the empire's most lucrative yet controversial commodities: slaves. Activities of smuggling slaves thrived, especially during times of war or in regions where slavery was more tightly controlled. Using hidden routes, smugglers who carried slaves aboard their ships were able to avoid Roman checkpoints. Once docked, they sold these unfortunate slaves in secret auctions.

Piracy in Ancient Rome

While smugglers were the champions of Roman black markets, pirates ruled the open seas. Piracy's roots stretched back before the rise of the Roman Empire. Since the earliest days of maritime trade, when merchant vessels began crossing the Mediterranean, piracy flourished as a dark counterpart to legitimate commerce. Some might agree that piracy is almost as old as seafaring itself. Records from ancient Egypt, Greece, and even Phoenicia talk about raids on ships and coastal settlements. Many may imagine pirates as lawless marauders—thanks to the cinema— however, they were far more than that. They were, in fact, skilled seamen and opportunists who were well versed in the complexities of maritime trade.

Of course, piracy was a persistent threat to Roman commerce, especially once Rome established its dominance over the Mediterranean, which the Romans referred to as Mare Nostrum. The waters surrounding Cilicia, Crete, and Sicily were notorious nests for pirates. Since these locations had rocky coastlines and many hidden coves, it was easy for pirates to launch surprise attacks on unsuspecting merchant ships.

Ever strategic opportunists, these pirates would only target vessels that carried the most valuable and heavily taxed goods. So, ships carrying Egyptian grain shipments, which were a need for ancient Romans, spices from the East, and silks from Asia became their main targets. However, goods were not the only things they would get their hands on. Pirates in the Roman era would also capture those aboard. They would either demand ransom or sell their captives into slavery in black markets across the empire.

What made the pirates so successful was the geography of the Mediterranean, corrupt local officials, and defiant yet ambitious merchants. Most of the time, these pirates operated in coordination with Roman elites who chose to turn a blind eye to their activities. In return for their ignorance, the pirates gave them a cut of their profits. The Roman state publicly condemned piracy, as it was seen as a major threat to the empire's economic stability. However, it was different in private; many within the government did not hesitate to earn benefits from the illegal spoils. Because of these greedy officials, pirates were able to receive insider information; they would know which ship to attack and which ones were laden with the most expensive cargo.

As piracy became rampant in Rome, harming both the republic itself and its allies, Marcus Antonius Orator (the grandfather of Mark Antony) was sent to deal with the pirates in 102 BCE. Antonius was able to suppress pirate activity in Cilicia, making the region safer again for Roman trade and shipping. His success was appreciated to the point where the Senate agreed to hold a naval triumph in his honor.

However, this was not the end of the piracy infestation in Rome. When the pirates loomed large again a few decades later, another figure was sent to the Mediterranean to undergo a pirate-hunting campaign. This time around, the responsibility was given to Marcus Antonius Creticus (the son of Marcus Antonius Orator and the father of Mark Antony) in 74 BCE. However, he failed to mirror his father's success.

After being bestowed with the title of proconsul, Antonius Creticus was tasked with eradicating pirates operating around Crete. Unfortunately, the campaign turned into a disaster. Seeing an opportunity for personal enrichment, he abused his power and plundered the provinces he was supposed to protect from the pirates. The Cretans, however, had secured allegiance with the pirates; after all, the island was the pirates' stronghold. They were able to defeat Antonius Creticus and his forces.

News of his failure was made known to everyone back in the Eternal City. He became a subject of ridicule among the Roman officials. They even sarcastically gave him the cognomen (third name of a Roman citizen) "Creticus," which means the conqueror of Crete.

The pirate threat grew only more dangerous and pervasive. Aside from the usual raids and plundering, piracy had become deeply entwined with the corruption that plagued the Roman elite. Even senators were not free from this tempting path to achieve immense wealth. Eager to expand their power and influence without having to go through the long journey, they hired pirates to carry out their dirty work.

It was only when Pompey the Great rose to prominence that the pirates finally met a formidable opponent. Already a military commander of immense skill with a growing reputation, the Romans had high hopes for Pompey to finally eradicate piracy once and for all. He wasted no time in launching a campaign in 67 BCE.

Perhaps what set Pompey apart from his predecessors was his strategic brilliance. By organizing the Mediterranean into various sectors and assigning different commanders to each region, he was able to create a powerful naval force to hunt down pirates. His ability to unite Rome's military might was indeed impressive. He was able to not only pursue the pirates on open seas but also strike them down at their own bases of operations.

Pompey never hesitated. He swiftly cut off pirate access to key trade routes and blockaded pirate ports. When the opportunity arose, he attacked the pirate fleets with overwhelming force. It took him only forty days to clear the western Mediterranean of pirate activity. He then turned his gaze to the eastern Mediterranean, where piracy was more deeply rooted.

Cilician pirates were undeniably more organized and powerful. Their strongholds and hideouts, which were located in rugged areas, made them hard to penetrate. However, Pompey was not one to easily back down. His decisive victory eventually came when he successfully defeated the pirates at their main base in Cilicia. He struck down dozens of pirates, and those who survived were taken prisoner. Now that the pirates' territory was seized, Pompey established a city he named Pompeiopolis to further secure the region.

The entire campaign of subduing pirates in the Mediterranean lasted for only three months. Knowing that there was a possibility for the pirates to rise again and threaten the republic once more, Pompey resorted to a more lenient and pragmatic approach after he was done with the campaign. Instead of executing or locking up each surviving pirate, he offered them a chance to start again. Those who agreed to surrender were allowed to resettle in Roman colonies with their families. This helped the Roman Republic in securing long-term stability.

Rome's trade routes were made safe again, and the grain supply was greatly restored. As for Pompey, his success in eliminating the pirate threat awarded him immense wealth and unimaginable fame. Today, he is known as one of Rome's greatest military commanders. Ironically, his own son, Sextus Pompey, would later be described by ancient historians as one of the most notorious pirates in Roman history, although Sextus might not have viewed himself as one.

Known in full as Sextus Pompeius Magnus Pius, he was the younger son of Pompey the Great. His story could also be a study of how a man born into prominence could be both praised and condemned by ancient Rome.

It all began with his father's defeat at the hands of Julius Caesar at the Battle of Pharsalus in 48 BCE. Pompey was once a champion of the Roman Republic and the mighty conqueror of the Mediterranean pirates, but he was left with no choice but to seek refuge under a foreign power. Perhaps desperate, the military commander put his trust in the young Egyptian pharaoh to protect him from Caesar's hunt. However, this trust was misplaced, and it cost him his life.

Pompey's death.[38]

With his father's unfair death, Sextus was forced into hiding. However, he was not planning on letting his father's legacy be stained. In Hispania, he fought Caesar's generals and built a reputation based on his success in guerilla warfare. Unfortunately for Sextus, Caesar's forces were strong, and he was eventually defeated. Despite being forced to flee again, he was determined to undo Caesar's carefully crafted story that depicted Pompey the Great as a defeated and irrelevant figure of the old republic. After Caesar's assassination, he gathered what remained of his father's supporters and began working on consolidating his power in the provinces where Pompey was held in high regard, particularly in Sicily and the surrounding areas.

The republic had always valued Sicily; it was considered Rome's breadbasket. In Sextus's mind, taking control of Sicily would grant him a firm foothold in the Mediterranean. He who controlled Rome's grain supply could either make or break the republic's stability. In other words, when Sextus seized Sicily, he effectively held Rome hostage.

His extraordinary fleet soon became a formidable force in the Mediterranean. He was supported by Pompey's loyalists and defectors from various factions who were against the Second Triumvirate (Mark Antony, Octavian, and Lepidus).

From his base in Sicily, Sextus launched naval raids against military convoys and Rome's commercial ships. Some may agree that his tactics mirrored those of the pirates his father had once fought against. However, Sextus did not view himself as one; he thought of himself as the rightful heir to Pompey the Great's cause. His father was the last defender of the Roman Republic, and he was proud to stand against the forces of tyranny led by the Second Triumvirate.

Sextus and his forces became so powerful that Octavian and Antony were forced to head to the negotiating table. The Treaty of Misenum was signed in 39 BCE, which allowed Sextus to control Sicily, Sardinia, and Corsica. This gave him legitimate power and de facto control over the western Mediterranean. In return for these terms, Sextus agreed to end his raids and unblock the grain supply to the Eternal City.

However, the treaty did not give Rome permanent peace. Octavian and Mark Antony never viewed Sextus as a legitimate ruler. Both saw him as a thorn in their sides. Octavian married Scribonia in 37 BCE. Since she was related to Sextus, the union was intended to reinforce the fragile peace. Yet, it did little. Octavian and Mark Antony signed the Treaty of Tarentum, which provided them with renewed military power. Antony himself provided ships to Octavian. Along with the leadership of Marcus Vipsanius Agrippa in his fleet, Octavian finally had the resources to challenge Sextus on the high seas. To Sextus, this was an invitation for a confrontation. He knew a war was on the horizon, so he resumed his naval blockade. Rome was cut off from its grain supply once more.

The Eternal City began to witness a scene of unrest when grain shortages became an issue. This forced Octavian to act. The future emperor launched an attack on Messina in 36 BCE, which was a key Sicilian stronghold controlled by Sextus. A full-scale naval war was set in motion. In the beginning, Sextus seemed to have gained the upper hand; using his superior fleet, he launched a series of counterattacks and struck at Octavian's supply lines. This was the very moment where many would suggest that Octavian was no match for Sextus on the open sea.

Fortunately for Octavian, he had Marcus Vipsanius Agrippa by his side. Regarded as one of Rome's most skilled military commanders and the future emperor's most trusted ally, the tides of war slowly changed. Agrippa made use of vessels equipped with *corvi* (grappling hooks) and *harpax* (a type of catapult-launched harpoon) to latch onto Sextus's ships. This reduced the mobility advantage of Sextus's fleet. Agrippa's men were also highly efficient in close combat, so they were well prepared for critical naval engagements.

Sextus was eventually defeated in the Battle of Naulochus in 36 BCE. Again, he fled to the Aegean Sea before making his way eastward, particularly to areas controlled by Mark Antony. Sextus knew that tensions were brewing between Mark Antony and Octavian. Thus, he hoped to get on Antony's good side and benefit from the political rivalry between the two. But, in the end, Sextus was captured by Mark Antony's own general, Marcus Titius. Titius was believed to have had a personal grudge against Sextus—he had killed Titius's father in an earlier conflict.

This was the end of the road for Sextus Pompey. He was executed in 35 BCE. Just as he had feared, his memory was deliberately tarnished by Octavian and the Augustan writers. Sextus held great importance in the politics and military of the republic, but he was reduced to a mere pirate. Instead of being a legitimate contender in the civil war, he was described by ancient historians and poets (especially those who supported Augustus) as nothing more than a nuisance who disrupted Rome's stability. Writers like Velleius Paterculus and Appian, for example, wrote him as little more than a brigand, dismissing his military prowess and downplaying the threat he posed. As for Augustus, this portrayal of Sextus served him well.

Chapter 10 – The Ghosts of Pompeii

The sun had just risen, shining its first ray of light over the cobbled streets of Pompeii. A man named Lucius was all ready for the day. Lucius, a modest yet well-respected merchant in the city, adjusted his tunic before stepping out of his villa. His home was typical of the Pompeian elite. It was a small domus yet comfortable enough for his family of four. It featured a courtyard adorned with delicate frescoes that narrated the stories of Roman gods and heroes. Lucius could smell the freshly baked bread made by the local baker right across from his villa. He took a whiff and continued his walk. He was accompanied by the salty breeze from the nearby Bay of Naples.

Life was relaxing in Pompeii. It was, after all, a popular coastal city for wealthy Romans seeking leisure and relaxation. However, Lucius's day was different from that of the aristocrats on vacation. His day was a healthy balance between work, social obligations, and personal indulgence.

As he got closer to the center of Pompeii, Lucius was greeted by the sounds of laborers pushing their carts filled with fruits, vegetables, and spices. Along the streets, one could find a line of shops complete with vendors hawking their goods. He made his way through the forum, the city's nucleus. It was a public square where events took place, ranging from political meetings to religious festivals to lively markets. Its amphitheater and theater were also among the largest in the Roman world, showcasing the city's love for entertainment and culture.

The forum was always alive, with people walking around and conducting business. The look of this location was a sight to behold; each corner featured statues of the city's benefactors all dressed in togas. It is safe to say that Pompeii was, in many ways, a reflection of the Eternal City itself, though it was smaller in scale.

The city of Pompeii was an important city in the empire. It was originally founded by the Oscans and later influenced by the Greeks and Etruscans. The city's greatest quality was its strategic location on the coast. Its close proximity to Naples made it an attractive destination for rich Romans. They often traveled to Pompeii for vacation and built luxurious villas overlooking the bay. However, Pompeii was not a provincial town reserved only for the wealthy. Since it flourished as a trade hub, receiving ships from all corners of the known world, the city was also a land of opportunity for the plebeians and freedmen. They could work and earn enough to live a decent life. Some might even get lucky enough to be able to climb up the Roman hierarchy. Lucius himself had risen from a modest background to become a respected merchant through his dealings in olive oil and textiles.

A short distance away from the forum, one could set eyes on one of Pompeii's most revered landmarks. Known as the Temple of Jupiter, it perched on a hill overlooking the bustling marketplace. The temple was dedicated to Jupiter (equivalent to Greek Zeus).

The ruins of the once glorious Temple of Jupiter.[39]

In the eyes of the Romans, Jupiter was not merely a divine being; he was the protector of the state, and his name was often called upon during political and military decisions. It should not come as a surprise that the Romans paid extra care in constructing the temple. Although its design was typical of Roman architecture (it bore a striking resemblance to the great Capitoline Temple in Rome), its grand flight of steps that led up to the main platform impressed anyone who laid eyes on it. The temple was also flanked by towering Corinthian columns, which featured exquisitely carved reliefs of mythological scenes, the most important one being an image of Jupiter's victories over the Titans.

Inside the temple was a grand statue of the god looming over the altar. His figure was imposing and majestic—fitting for his status as the king of the gods. The statues must have required a substantial amount of money and resources to be built. It was sculpted from marble and adorned with leaves made out of pure gold. Jupiter was depicted seated on his throne with a thunderbolt firmly held in one of his hands while the other held a scepter. The builders of the statue also carved Jupiter's eyes with such detail that the god appeared as if he was watching over the city.

Jupiter was accompanied by statues of his consort, Juno (the Greek Hera), and his daughter, Minerva (the Greek Athena)—these three deities made up the

A wall painting of Jupiter recovered from Pompeii.[40]

Capitoline Triad. Since Pompeii had been a Roman colony since 80 BCE, the city had adopted the worship of the Capitoline Triad as a central part of its identity. Because of this, temples in Pompeii were more than a place where religious ceremonies were held. The Temple of Jupiter was deeply tied to the city's civic life. Public speeches, political meetings, and even official proclamations often took place in front of the temple.

The temple was also a gathering place whenever the city was thrown into a crisis. Whenever there were natural disasters or military threats, the Pompeiians would flock to this temple, where they would offer sacrifices. This was done in hopes of appeasing Jupiter and securing his favor. Animal sacrifices were common. Bulls were often used, as they were believed to be the best choice to offer to the god of lightning.

When Lucius finally arrived at his store, he wasted no time in beginning his daily routine. He supervised his slaves and workers as they arranged the fine goods imported from vast provinces across the empire. Lucius had almost everything in his store; there were exquisite wines from Gaul, olive oil from Hispania, and unique glassware from Egypt. Once he was done checking his inventory, Lucius got himself ready for another walk.

This time, he made his way to the city's public baths. Spending some time in the public baths was an important relaxation ritual back then. The baths were where Romans would socialize. Senators, merchants, and craftsmen would gather around to discuss all sorts of matters, be it about the state of Roman politics and the emperor or even gossip about the elites. As for Lucius, he always had his ears open. The empire was full of intrigues, so it was always good to stay up to date on the whispers going around.

The Roman Baths at Bath, England.[41]

In the evening, Lucius attended a banquet hosted by his dear friend. He mingled with guests and feasted on roasted meats, fresh fish, and fruits. Soothing tunes filled the air, as talented musicians were hired to play their lyres and flutes. Amidst the crowd was an extremely wealthy patron who had spoken at length about his wish to sponsor a new gladiatorial game in the city. Lucius listened attentively. To the merchant, these games were not merely entertainment. Since the games would be hosted for weeks, crowds from across the region would come to Pompeii. Lucius's business would boom as a result.

However, little did they know that the gods had another plan for them, and subtle signs had already started to show. Occasionally, the ground would tremble. Lucius, like many others, had grown accustomed to these tremors; the Pompeiians often shrugged it off as nothing more than just a minor natural occurrence. The inhabitants went about their lives as usual—merchants would tend to their businesses while others would attend theatrical performances or socialize at the baths. They truly had no idea what Mother Nature would soon unleash upon them.

Pompeii with Mount Vesuvius in the background.[42]

At noon on August 24th, 79 CE, the first sign of catastrophe began to worry the Pompeiians. Mount Vesuvius had erupted with such force that a plume of ash, rock, and scorching-hot volcanic gasses rose high up in the sky. This could be seen by those living hundreds of miles away. The blast was sudden, and the towering column of ash and rock loomed over the region for hours, leading the Pompeiians to wonder whether this was an ominous sign sent by the gods.

As the column cooled, the dark soot began to drift back to earth. At first glance, it appeared to be fine-grained ash raining gently on the streets and covering the marble buildings of Pompeii like dust. The situation in the city was still calm. The citizens were confused, but they were also in awe since they had never witnessed this occurrence before. Unbeknownst to them, this was only the beginning. As the ash thickened, Pompeii witnessed chunks of pumice and other lightweight rocks falling from the sky. Before they knew it, roofs began to collapse, and statues lost their limbs.

A surge of panic hit the inhabitants of Pompeii. They had some time to flee, and many did. Many took their belongings before fleeing on foot. Some chose to take a boat and seek refuge in neighboring towns. As for Lucius, he quickly made his way back to his family, where they were already in the midst of packing their valuables. They could only hope that they were just in time to leave the city and save themselves. No one could predict that this was the prelude to one of the world's most terrifying natural disasters.

The Last Day of Pompeii by the Russian painter Karl Bryullov.[43]

The eruption was witnessed firsthand by Pliny the Elder, the famed Roman author of the first natural encyclopedia. He was stationed at

Misenum across the Bay of Naples. As the commander of a Roman fleet, Pliny was there to oversee naval operations. Since he was a scholar and a naturalist, Pliny's curiosity quickly took over the moment he saw the massive cloud rise from Vesuvius. Perhaps driven by his scientific instincts, he ordered his ships to sail toward the eruption. He intended to observe and study the phenomenon, but when he saw the danger people were in, he made it his mission to rescue the Romans trapped by the falling debris.

Unfortunately, the rescue operation went south. Pliny found it extremely difficult to navigate the waters as they approached the coast. This was largely due to the falling ash and pumice. While the sea churned with volcanic debris, the air was filled with toxic gasses. The sky turned dark, making it difficult for the crew to adjust their sight. Nevertheless, Pliny did not give up; he ordered his crew to press on. He was intent on saving those trapped in the towns around Pompeii.

But Mother Nature was not yet done. The closer they got to land, the worse their condition became. The air was suffocating, as sulfurous gasses burned their lungs. Pliny was overcome by the toxic fumes when he attempted to disembark and rescue survivors. The great scholar and commander died, succumbing to the very disaster he initially wished to investigate.

As for those trapped in Pompeii, their situation did not get any better. The rain of ash and pumice soon gave way to something far more deadly. The Pompeiians saw fast-moving surges of superheated gas and ash racing down the slopes of Vesuvius. Known as pyroclastic flows, they obliterated everything that stood in their path. The heat was so intense that flesh vaporized instantly when it came in contact with the volcanic matter. Those who perished left only their hardened forms.

Lucius and his family were among the many who managed to make their way into the streets. However, there was no way out. The air was thick with ash, and they could only see darkness. The ground continued to tremble as the pyroclastic flows neared. Lucius and the rest tried to find shelter, but everything had collapsed. Seeing that the end was near, Lucius held his family tightly as the torrent of ash and debris buried them. Their bodies were frozen in time, much like the rest of the city's inhabitants. In just a matter of hours, the once flourishing city was transformed into a graveyard, with victims entombed under layers of volcanic material.

Of course, Pompeii was not the only city that fell to the wrath of the volcanic eruption. Nearby towns like Herculaneum suffered a similar fate. While Pompeii was covered in ash and pumice, Herculaneum was buried under a thick layer of volcanic mud, which preserved buildings, organic materials, and even human remains.

John Martin's Destruction of Pompeii and Herculaneum.[44]

Interestingly, the horror that struck these cities was witnessed by another figure: Pliny the Younger. The nephew of Pliny the Elder, he was also stationed at Misenum when the disaster erupted. He was safe across the bay—a fate that was not shared with his uncle—yet the sight of the volcanic eruption was enough to terrify the Roman author. Pliny the Younger described the disaster in great detail when he wrote to the historian Tacitus. He told the historian of his feeling when he first saw the immense cloud of ash and gas rise higher as the seconds passed by. Pliny said he thought the world was coming to an end.

Because of Pliny's letters—though they were written years after the event—we get a detailed firsthand account of the eruption of Mount Vesuvius. He described the disaster as beginning with the appearance of a towering cloud in a shape that resembled the massive trunk of a pine tree (this is similar to what we call a mushroom cloud). Pliny also mentioned the bravery of his uncle and his tragic death in his letters.

Back in the Eternal City, the reaction was swift. The moment news of the eruption reached Emperor Titus, who had just ascended to the throne in the same year, he was quick to dispatch relief efforts to the region. The scale of the destruction undoubtedly shocked the empire. In the aftermath of the eruption, scholars agree that Rome lost at least sixteen thousand people. Pompeii was home to approximately eleven thousand to fifteen thousand inhabitants, and Herculaneum had a population of at least four thousand people. This eruption was one of the deadliest natural disasters to ever occur in the ancient world.

Titus was said to have personally overseen the distribution of aid. He even ordered a special investigation into the disaster. Nonetheless, despite his efforts, Pompeii and a few other towns never saw light again. They were never rebuilt and left forgotten. Pompeii was buried underneath layers of volcanic ash and pumice for nearly 1,700 years.

The rediscovery of Pompeii took place in 1748 when workers were digging for a foundation near the town of Resina (modern-day Ercolano). The discovery was more or less accidental, but it quickly garnered the attention of a Spanish military engineer named Roque Joaquín de Alcubierre. Working under the Bourbon King Charles III of Spain, Alcubierre was already familiar with stories of cities buried by the eruption. By the time of the discovery, the Spanish engineer was supervising the excavation of Herculaneum. Alcubierre quickly shifted his attention to the newly discovered site, marking the beginning of one of the most significant archaeological excavations in history.

Excavations were not an easy walk in the park. Workers had to clear away multiple layers of ash and rock that had been there untouched for centuries. However, once they were done, the city emerged almost perfectly preserved. It was as if time had been frozen. Buildings that did not collapse stood intact, complete with their elaborate frescoes and mosaics that adorned the walls. Archaeologists also discovered everyday objects, including tools, pottery, and various household items.

The most haunting discoveries were the bodies of the victims. When archaeologists poured plaster into the cavities left behind by the decayed bodies, they created eerily lifelike casts of people in their final moments. Some were crouching or lying down, while others died holding their family in a tight hug as the pyroclastic flows surged toward them. Many were clutching their most prized possessions, perhaps hoping to escape by sea and eventually start a new life in another town.

It is undeniable that the most remarkable aspect of the rediscovery was the city's state. Despite the eruption that had claimed the lives of many, Pompeii appeared almost exactly as it had almost two thousand years ago. It differs greatly from other archaeological sites around the globe, where structures and buildings were often corroded by the passage of time. Ironically, Pompeii was preserved by the very force that annihilated it. The ash and pumice that buried the city had sealed it off from the elements, protecting its structures, art, and artifacts from decay. Today, Pompeii is open to the public. Curious visitors can walk through the streets and enter the homes once resided by the ancient Romans. The city has essentially become a living museum, offering a window into the lives of those who lived during the flourishing empire.

The casts of victims in Pompeii.[45]

To this day, archaeologists and historians are still uncovering more about the daily lives of the Pompeiians before the disaster struck. Perhaps one of the most recent debates was about the actual date of the eruption of Mount Vesuvius. For centuries, scholars accepted the date of the eruption as sometime in August 79 CE. This was largely based on a letter written by Pliny the Younger. However, new evidence emerged that indicated that the eruption might have happened in a different month.

The discovery of preserved remains of fruits, including pomegranates and walnuts, indicates that the eruption likely occurred sometime between October and November, as it was impossible for these fruits to have ripened by August. The victims also wore clothing that was better suited for a cooler autumn day rather than a hot summer day. Other clues, such as a coin found in the ruins with markings dating to mid-September, have also led scholars to question the traditional date.

Regardless of the exact timing of the eruption, it is hard to dismiss that Pompeii's rediscovery provided us with a substantial understanding of the ancient world. The preserved remains of the victims and structures in the city give us clearer insights into their art, architecture, daily life, social structure, and the very nature of Roman urban existence.

Conclusion

Now that we have reached the end of the book, it is sufficient to say that Rome was far more than just its famed achievements. It is true that Rome is often celebrated and remembered for its glory, but its lesser-known episodes are just as captivating.

Through these forgotten stories, we are able to take a better glimpse of the empire. The Eternal City gave birth to a long list of powerful figures that history could never forget, yet the individuals explored in this book held equal importance to the shaping of the empire. They each had their own ways of navigating the treacherous path to power and, for some, to freedom. Descriptions of the daily lives of ordinary citizens tend to be removed from the majority of narratives of grand historical events. The citizens, from merchants to farmers and from craftsmen to entertainers, had a hand in shaping the social and economic structure of Rome.

People often speak of Rome's might, but beneath those triumphs lay many episodes of vulnerability. The Eternal City was constantly fraught with internal challenges. Economic strain, social unrest, and leadership crises were common sights that exposed the city's fragility. The natural world was also not merciful; fires, plagues, and earthquakes often shook the empire to its foundations. Even the Roman legions, often described to be invincible, were not free from defeat and disasters. Take the mysterious disappearance of the Ninth Legion as an example. Despite being feared for centuries, its theories of how it disappeared serve as striking evidence that Rome was not untouchable.

The history of Rome is extensive and complex. It spanned over a millennium, beginning from its legendary founding in 753 BCE to the fall of the Western Roman Empire in 476 CE. Its history covers centuries of wars, political affairs, conspiracies, and cultural transformations. To tell its story properly would require hundreds of pages, and even that would only scratch the surface of Rome's magnificence. Even so, these lesser-known stories offer a meaningful glimpse into the unique history of the empire. Although they might not include the most popular individuals and incidents, these stories provide readers with a small window into how the Romans once lived.

If you enjoyed this book, I'd greatly appreciate a review on Amazon because it helps me to create more books that people want. It would mean a lot to hear from you.

To leave a review:

1. Open your camera app.
2. Point your mobile device at the QR code.
3. The review page will appear in your web browser.

Thanks for your support!

Here's another book by Matt Clayton that you might like

MYTHOLOGY

A CAPTIVATING GUIDE TO GREEK MYTHOLOGY,
EGYPTIAN MYTHOLOGY, NORSE MYTHOLOGY,
CELTIC MYTHOLOGY AND ROMAN MYTHOLOGY

MATT CLAYTON

Free Bonus from Captivating History (Available for a Limited time)

Hi History Lovers!

Now you have a chance to join our exclusive history list so you can get your first history ebook for free as well as discounts and a potential to get more history books for free!

Simply visit the link below to join.

Or, Scan the QR code!

captivatinghistory.com/ebook

Also, make sure to follow us on Facebook, X, and YouTube by searching for Captivating History.

Bibliography

Addis, Ferdinand. "Rome: Eternal City." *Bloomsbury Publishing*, 2018.

Adhamy, Amir. "Agrippina the Younger: the first true empress of Ancient Rome." *HistoryExtra*, November 15, 2023. https://www.historyextra.com/period/roman/agrippina-younger-empress-ancient-rome-empress-nero-caligula/.

Andrews, Evan. "8 Things You May Not Know About Emperor Claudius." *History,* September 11, 2023. https://www.history.com/news/8-things-you-may-not-know-about-emperor-claudius.

Bileta, Vedran. "Agrippina the Younger: Rome's first true Empress." *TheCollector*, October 18, 2021. https://www.thecollector.com/agrippina-the-younger/.

Bileta, Vedran. "Caligula: 18 Facts on the 'Mad' Roman Emperor." *TheCollector*, August 16, 2023. https://www.thecollector.com/caligula/.

Dash, Mike. "King, Magician, General ... Slave: Eunus and the First Servile War Against Rome." *A Blast From the Past,* July 16, 2016. https://mikedashhistory.com/2016/07/16/king-magician-general-slave-eunus-and-the-first-servile-war-against-rome/.

Daugherty, Greg. "Was Commodus the Worst Emperor in Ancient Roman History?" *History,* August 18, 2022. https://www.history.com/news/commodus-worst-roman-emperor-gladiator.

De Abreu, Kristine. "Exploration Mysteries: Disappearance of the Ninth Legion." *Explorersweb,* March 8, 2023. https://explorersweb.com/exploration-mysteries-disappearance-of-the-ninth-legion/.

Dunn, Daisy. "The truth behind Ancient Rome's most controversial woman," *BBC,* May 7, 2021. https://www.bbc.com/culture/article/20210506-the-truth-behind-ancient-romes-most-controversial-woman.

Kings and Generals. "Before Spartacus: Second Servile War Against the Roman Republic," YouTube video, October 24, 2019. https://www.youtube.com/watch?v=jhLXhrOiLmk.

Mark, Joshua J. "The Spartacus Revolt." *World History Encyclopedia,* March 4, 2016. https://www.worldhistory.org/article/871/the-spartacus-revolt/.

Meddings, Alexander. "Messalina – the Empress Who Remarried While the Emperor Was Out of Town." *Walks Inside Rome,* accessed September 19, 2024. https://www.walksinsiderome.com/blog/messalina-the-empress-who-remarried-while-the-emperor-was-out-of-town/?fbclid=IwZXh0bgNhZW0CMTEAAR2RcEUXpvmZEx-Wgv9p6eJfIjRs1YWFXAmQeVdfAmW5svpsqsI3wKnL7to_aem_COQPsea OLhN_AwEFHhuoyQ.

Sullivan, Missy. "Pompeii" *History,* July 29, 2022. https://www.history.com/topics/ancient-rome/pompeii.

Wasson, Donald L. "Legio IX Hispana." *World History Encyclopedia,* July 16, 2021. https://www.worldhistory.org/Legio_IX_Hispana/.

Wasson, Donald L. "Livia Drusilla." *World History Encyclopedia,* May, 13, 2016. https://www.worldhistory.org/Livia_Drusilla/.

Wolfson, Aaron. "Julia Domna." *World History Encyclopedia,* September 18, 2020. https://www.worldhistory.org/Julia_Domna/

Wright, Jennifer. "Locusta of Gaul: Rome's Imperial Poisoner and Possibly the World's First Serial Killer," *CrimeReads.* November 2, 2021. https://crimereads.com/locusta-of-gaul-romes-imperial-poisoner-and-possibly-the-worlds-first-serial-killer/.

"Claudius." *PBS,* accessed September 9, 2024. https://www.pbs.org/empires/romans/empire/claudius.html#:~:text=Disfigured %2C%20awkward%20and%20clumsy%2C%20Claudius,women%20would%20p rove%20his%20undoing.

"Spartacus." *National Geographic,* accessed September 10, 2024. https://education.nationalgeographic.org/resource/spartacus/.

"The mystery of Rome's lost Ninth Legion: what really happened to them?," *History Skills,* accessed September 4, 2024. https://www.historyskills.com/classroom/ancient-history/ninth-legion/?srsltid=AfmBOorsceGcsIGCwlZ7gE9V7T4-xZZV91bguUkZ897nTOJhl4qGsnrc.

Image Sources

[1] https://commons.wikimedia.org/wiki/File:M443922_Julius-Caesar-taken-prisoner-by-Cilician-pirates-while-crossing-the-Aegean-Sea-c75-BC.jpg

[2] https://commons.wikimedia.org/wiki/File:RomanRepublic40BC.jpg

[3] https://commons.wikimedia.org/wiki/File:Cicero_Denounces_Catiline_in_the_Roman_Senate_by_Cesare_Maccari.png

[4] https://commons.wikimedia.org/wiki/File:CaesarRefusesTheDiademRidpathdrawing.jpg

[5] https://commons.wikimedia.org/wiki/File:Cleopatra_and_Caesar_by_Jean-Leon-Gerome.jpg

[6] Miguel Hermoso Cuesta, CC BY-SA 4.0 <https://creativecommons.org/licenses/by-sa/4.0>, via Wikimedia Commons:
https://commons.wikimedia.org/wiki/File:Livia_y_Tiberio_M.A.N._01.JPG

[7] Classical Numismatic Group, Inc. http://www.cngcoins.com, CC BY-SA 2.5 <https://creativecommons.org/licenses/by-sa/2.5>, via Wikimedia Commons:
https://commons.wikimedia.org/wiki/File:Caligula_sestertius_RIC_33_680999.jpg

[8] https://commons.wikimedia.org/wiki/File:Georges_Antoine_Rochegrosse_The_Death_of_Messalina_1916.jpg

[9] Carlos Delgado, CC BY-SA 3.0 <https://creativecommons.org/licenses/by-sa/3.0>, via Wikimedia Commons: https://commons.wikimedia.org/wiki/File:Ner%C3%B3n_y_Agripina.jpg

[10] José Luiz Bernardes Ribeiro: https://commons.wikimedia.org/wiki/File:Portrait_of_family_of_Septimius_Severus_-_Altes_Museum_-_Berlin_-_Germany_2017.jpg

[11] T8612, CC BY-SA 4.0 <https://creativecommons.org/licenses/by-sa/4.0>, via Wikimedia Commons: https://commons.wikimedia.org/wiki/File:First_Servile_War_(135-132_BC).png

[12] https://commons.wikimedia.org/wiki/File:Mario_vincitore_dei_Cimbri.jpg

[13] https://commons.wikimedia.org/wiki/File:Tod_des_Spartacus_by_Hermann_Vogel.jpg

[14] Fabien1309, CC BY-SA 2.0 FR <https://creativecommons.org/licenses/by-sa/2.0/fr/deed.en>, via Wikimedia Commons: https://commons.wikimedia.org/wiki/File:Statue-vercingetorix-jaude-clermont.jpg

[15] Modern portrayal of Roman soldiers (legionaries), CC0, via Wikimedia Commons: https://commons.wikimedia.org/wiki/File:Roman_holiday_birthplace_of_rome_roman_soldiers-883133.jpg!d.jpg

[16] Carole Raddato from FRANKFURT, Germany, CC BY-SA 2.0 <https://creativecommons.org/licenses/by-sa/2.0>, via Wikimedia Commons: https://commons.wikimedia.org/wiki/File:Statue_of_a_Gaulish_soldier_wearing_a_Celtic_torc_n ecklace,_Roman_clothes_and_holding_a_Gallic_shield,_most_likely_a_Gallic_aristocrat_recruit ed_into_the_Roman_auxiliaries,_Augustan_period_(50125723031).jpg

[17] Paul Walter, CC BY 2.0 <https://creativecommons.org/licenses/by/2.0>, via Wikimedia Commons: https://commons.wikimedia.org/wiki/File:Boudica_statue,_Westminster _(8433726848).jpg

[18] Yorkshire Museum, CC BY-SA 4.0 <https://creativecommons.org/licenses/by-sa/4.0>, via Wikimedia Commons: https://commons.wikimedia.org/wiki/File:Fragment_of_Legio_IX _Hispana_Tablet_YORYM_1998_21.jpg

[19] https://commons.wikimedia.org/wiki/File:Vincenzo_Camuccini_-_La_morte_di_Cesare.jpg

[20] Homoatrox, CC BY-SA 4.0 <https://creativecommons.org/licenses/by-sa/4.0>, via Wikimedia Commons: https://commons.wikimedia.org/wiki/File:Calig2en.png

[21] https://commons.wikimedia.org/wiki/File:The_Assassination_of_the_Emperor_Caligula.jpg

[22] https://commons.wikimedia.org/wiki/File:Robert,_Hubert_-_Incendie_%C3%A0_Rome_-.jpg

[23] https://commons.wikimedia.org/wiki/File:Marcus_Tullius_Cicero_dragged_from_his_l itter_and_assassinated_by_soldiers_under_the_command_of_Marc_Antony_43_BCE.jpg

[24] https://commons.wikimedia.org/wiki/File:Fulvia_y_Marco_Antonio,_o_La_venganza_de_ Fulvia_(Museo_del_Prado).jpg

[25] https://commons.wikimedia.org/wiki/File:Ostia_Antica_Mithraeum.jpg

[26] https://commons.wikimedia.org/wiki/File:Neuenheimer_Mithraeum.jpg

[27] https://commons.wikimedia.org/wiki/File:Mosaic_museum_Istanbul_2007_011.jpg

[28] https://commons.wikimedia.org/wiki/File:Gladiators_from_the_Zliten_mosaic_3.JPG

[29] https://commons.wikimedia.org/wiki/File:Jean-Leon_Gerome_Pollice_Verso.jpg

[30] Pascal Radigue, CC BY-SA 3.0 <https://creativecommons.org/licenses/by-sa/3.0>, via Wikimedia Commons: https://commons.wikimedia.org/wiki/File:Plan_Rome_ Caen_Circus_Maximus_Colis%C3%A9e.jpg

[31] https://commons.wikimedia.org/wiki/File:Jean_L%C3%A9on_G%C3%A9r%C3%B4me_- _Chariot_Race_-_1983.380_-_Art_Institute_of_Chicago.jpg

[32] https://commons.wikimedia.org/wiki/File:Proclaiming_claudius_emperor.png

[33] Chris 73, CC BY-SA 3.0 <https://creativecommons.org/licenses/by-sa/3.0>, via Wikimedia Commons: https://commons.wikimedia.org/wiki/File:Aqua_Claudia_05.jpg

[34] *my work, CC BY-SA 3.0 <https://creativecommons.org/licenses/by-sa/3.0>, via Wikimedia Commons: https://commons.wikimedia.org/wiki/File:Roman.Britain.campaigns.43.to.60.jpg*

[35] *https://commons.wikimedia.org/wiki/File:The_Emperor_Commodus_Leaving_the_Arena_at_the_Head_of_the_Gladiators_by_American_muralist_Edwin_Howland_Blashfield_(1848-1936)_01_(cropped).jpg*

[36] *Jofrey Rudel Marie-Lan Nguyen (Jastrow), CC0, via Wikimedia Commons: https://commons.wikimedia.org/wiki/File:COMMODE_HERCULE.jpg*

[37] *Jean-Pierre Dalbéra from Paris, France, CC BY 2.0 <https://creativecommons.org/licenses/by/2.0>, via Wikimedia Commons: https://commons.wikimedia.org/wiki/File:La_place_des_corporations_(Ostia_Antica)_(5900530118).jpg*

[38] *https://commons.wikimedia.org/wiki/File:Death_of_Pompey_Magnus.jpg*

[39] *Carla Brain, CC BY-SA 2.0 <https://creativecommons.org/licenses/by-sa/2.0>, via Wikimedia Commons: https://commons.wikimedia.org/wiki/File:Temple_of_Jupiter_(2).jpg*

[40] *https://commons.wikimedia.org/wiki/File:Zeus_pompei.JPG*

[41] *Diliff, CC BY-SA 3.0 <http://creativecommons.org/licenses/by-sa/3.0/>, via Wikimedia Commons: https://commons.wikimedia.org/wiki/File:Roman_Baths_in_Bath_Spa,_England_-_July_2006.jpg*

[42] *Qfl247, CC BY-SA 3.0 <https://creativecommons.org/licenses/by-sa/3.0>, via Wikimedia Commons: https://commons.wikimedia.org/wiki/File:Pompeii%26Vesuvius.JPG*

[43] *https://commons.wikimedia.org/wiki/File:Karl_Brullov_-_The_Last_Day_of_Pompeii_-_Google_Art_Project.jpg*

[44] *https://commons.wikimedia.org/wiki/File:Destruction_of_Pompeii_and_Herculaneum.jpg*

[45] *Lancevortex, CC BY-SA 3.0 <http://creativecommons.org/licenses/by-sa/3.0/>, via Wikimedia Commons: https://commons.wikimedia.org/wiki/File:Pompeii_Garden_of_the_Fugitives_02.jpg*

Printed in Dunstable, United Kingdom